2020 Sequoyah High School Masterlist

MXYA

VERY, VERY, VERY
DREADFUL

Also by Albert Marrin

Black Gold: The Story of Oil in Our Lives

FDR and the American Crisis

Flesh & Blood So Cheap: The Triangle Fire and Its Legacy
A National Book Award Finalist

Thomas Paine: Crusader for Liberty

Uprooted: The Japanese American Experience During World War II
A Sibert Honor Book

A Volcano Beneath the Snow: John Brown's War Against Slavery

VERY, VERY, VERY
DREADFUL

The Influenza Pandemic of 1918

Albert Marrin

Alfred A. Knopf ⟡ New York

THIS IS A BORZOI BOOK PUBLISHED BY ALFRED A. KNOPF

Text copyright © 2018 by Albert Marrin

All rights reserved. Published in the United States by Alfred A. Knopf,
an imprint of Random House Children's Books, a division of
Penguin Random House LLC, New York.

Knopf, Borzoi Books, and the colophon are registered trademarks of
Penguin Random House LLC.

For picture credits, please see page 191.

Visit us on the Web! randomhouseteens.com

Educators and librarians, for a variety of teaching tools, visit us at RHTeachersLibrarians.com

Library of Congress Cataloging-in-Publication Data is available upon request.
ISBN 978-1-101-93146-2 (trade) — ISBN 978-1-101-93147-9 (lib. bdg.) —
ISBN 978-1-101-93148-6 (ebook)

The text of this book is set in 12-point Granjon.

MANUFACTURED IN CHINA
January 2018
10 9 8 7 6 5 4 3 2 1

First Edition

This may serve to describe the dreadful condition of that day, though it is impossible to say anything that is able to give a true idea of it to those who did not see it, other than this, that it was indeed very, very, very dreadful, and no such tongue can express.

—Daniel Defoe, *A Journal of the Plague Year,* 1722

CONTENTS

VERY, VERY, VERY
DREADFUL

THE GREAT-GRANDDADDY OF THEM ALL

If you are in the business of infectious disease epidemics,
you can't ignore the 1918 flu—it's the great-granddaddy of them all.
—Dr. Donald Burke, Johns Hopkins Bloomberg School of
Public Health, 2004

Monday, March 11, 1918. Fort Riley, north-central Kansas. On a vast wind-swept plain covering more than 20,000 acres, scores of barracks, staff buildings, warehouses, repair shops, stables, and tent cities dotted the grounds. Rumor had it that ghosts roamed the parade ground on nights of the full moon, when coyotes howled. Fort Riley was home to the Seventh Cavalry, the unit that, forty-two years earlier, Colonel George Armstrong Custer had led to fight the Sioux and Cheyenne during the Indian wars.

That late-winter day in 1918 dawned cold and gray. Army recruits shivered, for, one wrote his folks, "barracks and tents were overcrowded and inadequately heated, and it was impossible to supply the men with sufficient warm clothing." To make matters worse, sand blown by gale-force winds stung bare skin and got into eyes and mouths, crunching between teeth. It had, some said, the faint smell of manure. Though Fort Riley had scores of motor vehicles, the U.S. army still used thousands of horses and mules to haul supplies. The animals left manure all over, which cleanup squads raked into piles, waist-high, for burning every few weeks. Two days earlier, work details had burned several hundred tons of the stuff with fuel oil. The fires gave off a foul yellowish haze, the wind scattering the powdery ashes into the sleeping quarters and mess halls.[1]

Recruits had swarmed into Fort Riley because their government sent them there. A savage war had been raging for nearly four years, since July 1914. Then called the Great War or the World War, today we know it as World War I or the First World

Fort Riley, Kansas. (c. 1918-1919)

War. Mainly, it was a struggle for power in Europe and for overseas colonies, raw materials, and markets. Two groups of nations fought. On one side stood the Central Powers, led by Germany and including Austria-Hungary, Bulgaria, and the Ottoman Empire, ruled by the Turks. Opposing them were the Allies, primarily the British Empire, France, Russia, and Italy. Though waged chiefly in Western Europe, the war spilled into nearly every corner of the globe.

Neutral at first, American public opinion gradually tilted in favor of the Allies. With the world's largest economy, the United States needed to trade its manufactured goods to prosper. But when Britain's Royal Navy blockaded Germany's seaports, cutting off overseas supplies of food and raw materials, Germany retaliated, unleashing its submarines to

keep vital supplies from reaching the Allies. After German U-boats ("undersea boats," or submarines) torpedoed American cargo ships, Congress declared war in April 1917.

Even though the United States was the world's industrial leader, its 378,000-strong army was tiny compared to the millions of men fielded by the European powers. A latecomer to the war, the United States was embarrassingly short of modern weapons, many of which it had to buy or borrow from the Allies. America's chief advantage was its manpower. Within days of the declaration of war, the nation set about creating an army of more than 4.7 million men, the largest in its history until then. Basic infantry training would take place in thirty-two camps across the country, and in dozens of facilities where specialized skills such as artillery, military engineering, and flying airplanes would be taught. Fort Riley's training area, called Camp Funston, held 56,000 recruits, making it the largest camp in the country.[2]

Among the recruits was Private Albert Gitchell, a mess cook. Before daybreak on March 11, 1918, Gitchell awoke feeling achy, his throat raw,

as if scoured with hot sandpaper. Too sick to prepare breakfast for his company, he dragged himself to Hospital Building 91. The orderly on duty took the private's temperature and promptly put him to bed with a "bad cold." But then a strange thing happened. Moments after Gitchell's head hit the pillow, Corporal Lee W. Drake appeared with the same complaint. Others quickly followed. By noon, 107 men had been admitted to the hospital with "bad colds." And that was just the beginning: within two weeks, a total of 1,127 men had been stricken. Upon closer examination, doctors decided they had an influenza outbreak—a local flare-up of an infectious disease—on their hands.

Influenza! Influenza! Just let the word slide off your tongue; it has such a mellow sound. Yet its history is anything but mellow. The name comes from the Italian *influenza coeli,* meaning "influence of the heavens," for Italian scientists in the 1600s thought meteors, comets, and the position of the planets shaped events on Earth. A century later, English speakers borrowed the Italian word; *flu* is simply a shortened form of *influenza*. The French called it *la grippe,* from *gripper,* "to grasp or hook," because the infection grabs hold of its victims.

Influenza outbreaks were usually an annual winter event in the Northern Hemisphere. Always a nuisance, flu sickened many but was gone after a few days of misery. Before 1918, most people, including physicians, were blasé about flu, accepting it as an expected part of life, to be endured, along with taxes and toothaches. "Influenza," the *New York Times* reported in 1901, "has apparently become domesticated with us."[3]

The disease's early symptoms resemble those of the common cold, only more severe: fever, cough, runny nose, muscle aches, fatigue. Harvey Cushing, a brilliant brain surgeon, caught *la grippe* in December 1906. Cushing described the ordeal in his diary: "Of all the depressing, rotten maladies this takes the cake, and I wonder that anyone had been able to stand being under the same roof with me for a week. One's many bad qualities surge to the surface and among them the cardinal symptoms of the disease may be . . . quarrelsomeness, irritability, loss of memory, despon-

dency . . . and a hopelessness of spirit. *Don't get it.*"[4]

Nevertheless, influenza was not a "reportable disease," a disease that, by law, physicians and hospitals must report to the local board of health. Reportable diseases include measles and diphtheria, killers especially of young children. Yet, unlike the common cold, which almost never causes death, seasonal flu can and does kill, though seldom in large numbers in relation to population size. Nowadays, the disease claims, on average, 36,000 Americans each year, out of a population of 320 million. Contrast this with another number: 35,092 Americans died in motor vehicle accidents in 2015. Worldwide, seasonal flu infects up to a billion people, killing up to half a million of these.[5]

What happened at Fort Riley, however, was more than a seasonal outbreak. As time would tell, it was merely the start of the mildest of three influenza waves that seemed to roll in out of nowhere. In the summer of 1918, the second wave struck as a highly contagious and lethal *epidemic,* an illness that races through a community, attacking many people at once. Worse yet, within weeks the epidemic exploded into a *pandemic,* an illness that travels rapidly from one continent to another, spreading worldwide, sickening and killing millions.

Flu pandemics are nothing new. Medical historians think the first one struck in 1510, infecting Asia, Africa, Europe, and the New World. Between the years 1700 and 1900, there were at least sixteen pandemics, some of them killing up to one million people. Yet these were tame compared to the 1918 calamity. It was by far the worst thing that has ever happened to humankind; not even the Black Death of the Middle Ages comes close in the number of lives it took. A 1994 report by the World Health Organization pulled no punches. The 1918 pandemic, it said, "killed more people in less time than any other disease before or since." It was the "most deadly disease event in the history of humanity." Other scientists called it "the greatest medical holocaust in history."[6]

The numbers are mind-boggling.

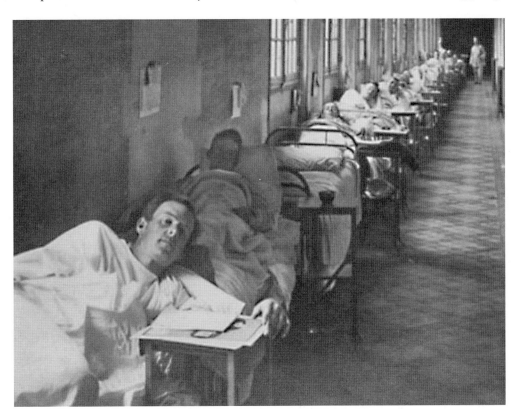

Crowded hospital corridors were a common sight at the height of the 1918 epidemic.

No other disease, no war, no natural disaster, no famine comes close to the great pandemic. In the space of eighteen months in 1918–1919, about 500 million people, one-third of the human race at the time, came down with influenza. The exact total of lives lost will never be known. An early estimate, made in 1920, claimed 21.5 million died worldwide. Since then, researchers have been continually raising the number as they find new information. Today, the best estimate of flu deaths in 1918–1919 is between 50 million and 100 million worldwide, and probably closer to the latter figure.[7]

Russia's Communist tyrant Joseph Stalin liked to say: "One death is a tragedy; the death of millions is a statistic." By that, Stalin—a wholesale murderer in his own right—meant that we are able to personalize another individual's suffering, feeling it as he or she does, but an enormous calamity, striking tens of millions, has a numbing effect. It is too awful for the mind to grasp and thus strikes us as merely a cold statistic, a number that blends individuals into a mass. Yet behind each individual is the tragedy of loved ones lost, a broken family, hardship, and sadness.

So it was with the 1918 pandemic. I know. My grandfather left Russia in 1913 to open a dry-goods shop in Cape Town, South Africa, planning to send for the family once the business got going. It was not to be. World War I came, and the flu took him; he lies in an unmarked grave.

My father, then sixteen, was drafted into the Red Army during the Russian Civil War. While he was fighting in Siberia, the flu struck him, too. Pa used to tell how, burning with fever, he went by horse-drawn sled to a hospital set up in a barn smelling of manure. The place was full, and he had to wait on a stretcher until a bed "opened"—that is, until a patient died. One soon did. Pa saw orderlies take the body away—then they put him to bed without changing the dirty sheets. The medical staff fed him beet soup and gave him glasses of vodka, a strong liquor. That was it. In 1918, even the best doctors knew nothing about what caused influenza, why it was so deadly, and how it spread. Tragically, medical science could not shorten the pandemic by so much as a day, or cure a single case. Pa's survival made him believe in God.

Today, we have a better, but not a full, understanding of what happened a century ago. Scientists agree that World War I and influenza joined together to make a bad situation worse. In a sense, the pandemic was nature's war on humanity, amid a war waged by humanity against itself. The wretched conditions in the training camps and on the fighting fronts created an ideal environment for the disease. These conditions allowed the influenza virus to mutate—change—into the "devil virus." Influenza, too, shaped the final stages of the war by influencing military operations, troop strength, and morale.[8]

On average, 2,250 soldiers a day were killed on the front in Western Europe. In total, over 9 million men lost their lives fighting on all fronts, and about 21 million civilians died as a direct result of the war. These are huge numbers. But if we assume 100 million influenza deaths, the disease killed at least three times as many people as the conflict itself.

Compare this to AIDS, the scourge of the late twentieth century. In just four months at the height of the pandemic—August through November 1918—influenza took more lives than AIDS did in thirty-nine years—that is, 78 million between 1975 and 2014.[9]

In the United States, influenza death rates were so high that the average life span fell by twelve years, from fifty-one in 1917 to thirty-nine in 1918. If you were a "doughboy"—slang for an American soldier—you had a better chance of dying in bed from flu or flu-related complications than from enemy action. After the war, the War Department listed 50,280 U.S. combat deaths; around 227,000 doughboys were hospitalized for battle wounds, and 340,000 for flu, of whom 51,164 died.[10]

A milder third wave began in late 1918, but the pandemic did not fade away for good until 1920. It is not very well known today. Though every nation has memorials to its World War I dead, no nation (that I know of) has any to its flu victims or the valiant men and women who gave their lives caring for them.

Scientists who study influenza today agree on the need for vigilance against future pandemics. Yet we cannot accomplish this without seeing the 1918 pandemic in a broader context. For it was part of a larger story, one going back many thousands of years, to before the dawn of civilization. The story is complicated. Like a mass of intertwined plant roots, the roots of the 1918 outbreak lie deep in the natural world, the history of science, and the sweeping arc of human history.

I cannot say it is a happy story or a pretty one; I admit that researching the pandemic gave me the blues at times. Often terrible, it illustrates how quickly an advanced civilization can begin to unravel in the face of a baffling affliction. An old proverb says: "Knowledge is power." It is, and that is why I have written this book. We need to look backward so we can look forward. We must understand what happened a century ago so we can better face facts and better defend ourselves when the next pandemic strikes, as scientists believe it surely will.

I

THE PITILESS WAR

Infectious disease is one of the great tragedies of living things—
the struggle for existence between different forms of life. . . .
Incessantly the pitiless war goes on, without quarter or armistice.
—Hans Zinsser, *Rats, Lice and History,* 1935

VISITORS FROM THE DEEP PAST

For untold generations, before the invention of written history, people lived in small family groups numbering, at most, a few dozen members. Our distant ancestors were merely creatures among other creatures, struggling to survive in an untamed wilderness. Called "hunter-gatherers" by modern social scientists, they were nomads, wanderers, people without a fixed place to live or call home. Each group had little contact with other groups, going from place to place, hunting animals and gathering roots, nuts, berries, and fruits to eat.

Unable to preserve or store food, nomads had to move continually, and on foot, to find their next meal. Without the wheel, a later invention, they also lacked draft animals; in fact, they kept no animals, except dogs, used for hunting and, in a pinch, for a meal. They carried their few possessions strapped

A Neolithic cave painting discovered in Spain.

to their backs or lashed between two wooden poles, which the women dragged along the ground. The men walked ahead, armed with clubs, stone-tipped spears, and bows and arrows, eyes peeled for danger or for game to pursue. Camps usually were just overnight stops to eat and sleep. But if the hunting in an area was good, the group might stay for a few days longer to butcher a kill, fill their bellies, and rest up for the trek ahead.

Hunting accidents, falls from trees, feuds within a group or with other groups took a steady toll. Still, the nomadic lifestyle had one advantage: it limited the impact of infectious diseases carried by animals.

All types of living beings have diseases that afflict them alone. Some-times, however, a disease attacking one life-form "crosses over" and infects another life-form. Ancient nomads did not live amid heaps of rubbish, their own waste, and polluted water. After a few days or weeks at a campsite, they moved on, leaving behind any disease-causing microbes that might be around. If a disease crossed over to, say, a hunter, he might die. The disease might even infect the entire group, killing every-one. But that would be the end of the disease; it stopped when there was no one left to infect. It could flour-ish only by becoming a "crowd dis-ease," infecting a population large enough to allow victims to pass it to the healthy.[1]

About 11,000 years ago, humankind reached a critical turning point. Across the world, big game animals—mastodons, giant sloths, and saber-toothed tigers—became extinct, probably because of over-killing by the hunters themselves. Naturally, as food became scarcer, nomads sought other ways of feeding themselves. Many began to experiment, growing wild plants like wheat, barley, and rice for food. They also learned to domesticate wild animals—that is, to tame and raise them. Cattle, horses, oxen, sheep, goats, pigs, ducks, geese, and chickens: all became important food sources, and some, like horses and oxen, became working animals.

This turning point, called the Agricultural Revolution, placed new demands on people. Above all, it required the cooperation of several groups living close together. Of necessity, hunter-gatherers settled into permanent communities when they took up farming. With a larger, more reliable food supply, their numbers grew. Over the centuries, individual farms linked up to form villages, villages grew into towns, and towns into cities. The first cities arose in the fertile valleys of the Tigris and

An artist's rendition of a farming settlement at Clegyr Boia (on what is today St. David's Peninsula, Pembrokeshire, Wales), about 4000 B.C.

Euphrates rivers in what is today Iraq, and along the Nile River in Egypt, the Indus River in India, and the Yellow River in China. Farming and cities later emerged in the New World, chiefly in Peru and Mexico, based on crops like maize and potatoes.

Civilization is the product of cities. Farmers usually grew more food than they needed, and the surplus gave others the leisure to do other things. Craftspeople, artists, priests, architects, engineers, and astronomers thrived. Over the centuries, they invented writing and mathematics, studied the sky, and created the calendar, which enabled farmers to plant and harvest at just the right times. Eventually, rulers raised armies and built empires to expand their domains.

The Agricultural Revolution, however, was a mixed blessing. Scientist and author Jared Diamond has even called it "the worst mistake in the history of the human race." Agriculture, Diamond argues, was harmful to health in several ways. Archaeologists—scientists who study early peoples through their physical remains and the things they built—have found that more food did not always mean better nutrition. Preserved teeth and bones show that the common people, the vast majority, were less healthy than their hunter-gatherer ancestors. A largely plant-based diet is high in sugars and starches but low in proteins, the chemical building blocks of life. This meant that the masses of farm folk were shorter than their ancestors—down from an average of five feet nine to five feet three for men and from five feet five to five feet one for women. Hunter-gatherers also lived longer, up to about forty years. Because of their diet and many hours of strenuous work, farmers were usually old at twenty-five and dead by thirty.[2]

Yet there were other culprits. To clear the land for planting, farmers cut down forests, plowed the soil, and dug irrigation canals. These activities displaced native bacteria from their environments, where they were harmless to humans, and created pools of stagnant water, breeding places for disease-carrying mosquitoes. Irrigation canals also allowed microscopic worms such as blood flukes to enter the body of anyone

Oxen pull a plow during planting season in a painting from the tomb of Sennedjem, in Deir el-Medina, on the west bank of the Nile River in Egypt. (c. 1290–1213 B.C.)

who walked in them barefoot. Dried worm eggs have been found in Egyptian mummies 3,000 years old.[3]

Farm settlements became magnets for infectious diseases in other ways. Grain mills and storehouses attracted hordes of rats, mice, and insects. To make matters worse, farmers lived close to their animals—close to their feces, urine, blood, breath, blisters, vomit, sweat, sores, spittle, and snot. To discourage thieves, they might bring prized animals into their homes. Farmers also collected human and animal waste to spread on their fields as fertilizer or to use in tanning hides into leather. Thus, by forcing people and animals to live close together, the Agricultural Revolution created ideal conditions for crowd diseases to take hold.

Close contact enabled the microbes that cause certain animal diseases to cross over to human hosts; *hosts* are living beings, animal or plant, on which or in which another organism lives. Today, we share no fewer than 300 diseases with domesticated animals. For example, humans get 45 diseases from cattle, including tuberculosis; 46 from sheep and goats; 42 from pigs; 35 from horses, including the common cold; and 26 from poultry. Rats and mice carry 33 diseases to humans, including bubonic plague. Sixty-five diseases, including measles, originated in man's best friend, the dog. We can still get parasitic worms from pet dogs and cats. That is why it is not a good idea to kiss a pet on the mouth or sleep with it in bed.[4]

Enclosed by high stone walls, with houses jammed close together along narrow streets, ancient cities were even more prone to crowd diseases than farms. Sanitation services did not exist, and drains flowed into the cobblestone gutters. City dwellers threw human waste into the streets, where it rotted, stank, and attracted vermin. Gutters ran with urine and liquefied manure. Stockyards and animal holding pens, usually located in crowded neighborhoods, swarmed with flies, fleas, and lice. Butchers slaughtered animals outdoors, in front of their shops, leaving puddles of blood; wastes like brains and guts wound up in streams used for washing and drinking. So it is no surprise that, for thousands of years,

animal-borne diseases killed more city dwellers than were born each year. For that reason, cities needed a steady influx of immigrants from the countryside to bolster their populations. Country folk came seeking adventure and opportunity.

CIVILIZATION'S PLAGUES

All ancient civilizations suffered from infectious diseases that crossed over from animals. The Old Testament tells how the Lord threatened to send plagues to the Egyptians unless Pharaoh, the ruler of Egypt, released the Hebrews from bondage. When Pharaoh refused to change his mind, the Almighty caused "sores that break into pustules on man and beast."[5] Pus is a yellow-white fluid that the body produces during infection; it consists of dead white blood cells and bacteria.

The first detailed description of an urban plague comes from ancient Greece. In 430 B.C., the city-state of Athens went to war with the city-state of Sparta. When the Spartan army invaded Athenian territory, thousands of farmers from outlying villages fled to the fortified city with their livestock. Already overcrowded

The Plague of Athens, a line engraving by James Fittler. (1811)

and filthy, Athens became even more so. Within days of the refugees' arrival, a disease more terrible than anything ever experienced broke out. The historian Thucydides, an eyewitness, described how Athenians died horribly, the sickness beginning with "violent heats in the head," followed by furious coughing, bloody vomiting, and finally severe diarrhea. The Plague of Athens killed young and old, slaves and freemen, generals and common soldiers. "The bodies of dying men lay one upon another, and half-dead creatures reeled about the streets and gathered round all the fountains in their longing for water," Thucydides wrote. By the time the plague ended in 427 B.C., one in three Athenians had perished.[6]

Modern scientists have not determined the cause of the sickness. Whatever it was, it set the pattern for future mass disease events. As it raged, hysteria spread, the Athenian economy collapsed, family loyalties broke down, friends abandoned friends, and many expected the end of the world. The medical profession stood by, puzzled and helpless. In desperation, physicians devised "preventatives" and "cures," which had no effect. The idea was to seem to know what to do—to do something, no matter how absurd, to *try*.

Centuries later, the capital of a vast empire also suffered from a mysterious plague. Rome, jam-packed with people and animals, was a city of luxurious villas of the rich and three-story apartment houses packed with the poor, the overwhelming majority. Disease was a regular visitor, even to the wealthy. The worst outbreak, known as the Antonine Plague, lasted on and off from A.D. 166 to 180. At its height, the disease took 2,000 Roman lives a day. It buried two emperors and wiped out nearby farming communities. Modern scientists are uncertain about its cause, except that it surely spread to people from domesticated animals.[7]

Dreadful as the Plague of Athens and the Antonine Plague were, they did not compare to the Plague of Justinian. Named for the emperor Justinian, who ruled the eastern part of the Roman Empire, it began in Constantinople (today's Istanbul, Turkey). From there, between A.D. 542 and 547, it swept across the European and African lands bordering the Mediterranean Sea.

Constantinople saw the first recorded outbreak of bubonic plague. *Bubonic* comes from the term *buboes*—swollen, inflamed lymph nodes as big as hens' eggs that appear on a victim's neck, groin, and armpits. Symptoms include high fever, pounding headache, delirium, and foul-smelling pus that escapes when a bubo bursts on its own or when a surgeon cuts it open. Often blood vessels rupture and blood leaks under the skin, forming black bruises, thus the plague's other name: the Black Death.

The disease originated somewhere in Central Asia, moving along the trade routes connecting Asia to the West. It is caused by *Yersinia pestis,* a rod-shaped bacterium that lives in the guts of fleas. The fleas, in turn, live on rodents, particularly rats. Rats are key, because they infest people's homes, barns, and storehouses. Fleas feed on blood, and when an infected flea bites a rat, it injects its bacteria-tainted saliva. Before long, the infected rat dies of plague; dead rats lying in the open are sure signs that plague is in an area. Like those of all warm-blooded animals, rats' bodies cool after death. Since fleas hate

HOW THE BUBONIC PLAGUE WAS TRANSMITTED

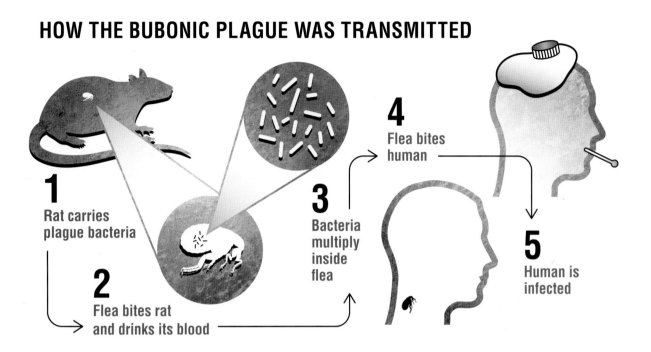

1 Rat carries plague bacteria

2 Flea bites rat and drinks its blood

3 Bacteria multiply inside flea

4 Flea bites human

5 Human is infected

cold, they seek other, living rats to live on and bite. If none are available, they settle for the next best thing—humans.[8]

The Plague of Justinian blazed through Constantinople like fire in dry grass. One survivor, the historian Procopius, claimed that some 10,000 people died each day—so many that gravediggers could not keep up with burials. In desperation, Emperor Justinian had the roofs of the stone towers that were built at intervals along the city's walls torn off and corpses thrown in, filling each in turn. Procopius recalled, "The whole human race came near to being annihilated. . . . [The plague] embraced the entire world, and blighted the lives of all men." Constantinople's best physicians were stumped, for "in this disease there was no cause which came within the province of human reasoning . . . [and] no device was discovered by man to save himself." The epidemic finally ended, no doubt because it ran out of vulnerable victims.[9]

Bubonic plague did not return for another eight centuries. The new

In a painting by Josse Lieferinxe, Saint Sebastian pleads for the life of an afflicted gravedigger during the sixth-century Plague of Justinian. (c. 1493–1508)

first cities, people threw garbage and wastewater out their windows; as a courtesy, they might shout to pedestrians, "Heads up!" or "Look out below!" Paris, continental Europe's largest and grandest city, stank like a latrine. We get a hint of this from an odd fact: Parisians named streets for human waste. *Merde,* French slang for "excrement," described reality. There was the rue Merdeux, rue Merdelet, rue Merdusson, and rue des Merdons—Street of Turds. Paris also had the rue du Pipi—Piss Street.[10]

The royal palaces were no cleaner than the city streets. Since there were no latrines in the Louvre (today a famous art museum), noble visitors relieved themselves on the marble floors and under the grand stairways. To mask odors, the wealthy used perfume and wore small bags of dried flower petals around their necks. From the king on down, everyone had fleas. Some aristocratic ladies held small dogs on their laps to draw fleas away from their own bodies. Rats scurried about as if they owned the French capital and its magnificent buildings.

epidemic, the worst yet, seems to have begun in China around the year 1342, then spread westward along overland trade routes and by sailing ship. From 1347 to 1352, it surged across the continent of Europe, reaching every country.

Fourteenth-century European cities were pestholes—filthy, animal-filled, and rat-infested. As in the

The Black Death killed about one-third, or 27 million, of Europe's

80 million inhabitants. Ignorant of its cause, people became confused, terrified, and vicious when it struck. Jews, a long-persecuted religious minority, became scapegoats, facing wholesale murder at the hands of frenzied mobs. Many Christians saw the plague as a sign of God's wrath directed at sinful humanity. The following lines were written around 1370 by an English parish priest named William Langland in his famous poem *Piers Plowman:*

> *Nature killed many through*
> *   corruptions,*
> *Death came driving after her and*
> *   dashed all to dust,*
> *Kings and knights, emperors and*
> *   popes,*
> *He left no man standing, whether*
> *   learned or ignorant;*
> *Whatever he hit stirred never*
> *   afterwards,*
> *Many a lovely lady and their*
> *   lover-knights*
> *Swooned and died in sorrow of*
> *   Death's blows. . . .*
> *For God is deaf nowadays and*
> *   will not hear us,*
> *And for our guilt he grinds good*
> *   men to dust.*[11]

In Central Europe and Germany, devout men sought divine mercy by becoming "flagellants." Crowds of these men roamed the countryside, each of them carrying a whip studded with bits of jagged metal. Upon reaching a town, they chanted prayers, stripped naked, and whipped themselves in imitation of Christ's Passion. An eyewitness wrote, "[They] lashed themselves viciously on their naked bodies until the blood flowed, while crowds, now weeping now singing, shouted 'Save us!'" Elsewhere, street artists covered walls with life-size drawings of the danse macabre, the "dance of

A dance of death etching from *The Nuremberg Chronicle* by Hartmann Schedel. (1493)

death." These portrayed grinning skeletons playing musical instruments, forcing the living to dance with them toward an open grave. According to the Italian merchant Agnolo di Tura, "All believed that it was the end of the world." Though the main epidemic ended in 1352, it was a rare year in the Middle Ages in which the Black Death did not strike somewhere in Europe.[12]

During this time, fear of the end of the world was a constant theme in European art. The German artist Albrecht Dürer portrayed the idea in his now-famous woodcut—a print made from a drawing cut into a block of wood—from 1498. Titled *The Four Horsemen of the Apocalypse,* the print illustrates a passage from the Bible (Revelation 6:1–8). The first rider carries a bow and arrows, symbolizing conquest. The second rider wields a sword, representing war. The third rider has an empty scale, a sign of famine. In the foreground rides Death with a trident to trample commoners and a bishop into the underworld.

The Great Plague of London, Europe's last serious outbreak of bubonic plague, occurred in 1665. We know a great deal about this event thanks to Daniel Defoe (1660–1731). Now known as the creator of the English novel, Defoe is the author of *Robinson Crusoe* (1719), which is still enjoyed by readers the world over. Also still in print is his narrative *A Journal of the Plague Year* (1722), written as though it were an eyewitness report.

The Four Horsemen of the Apocalypse by Albrecht Dürer. (1498)

Defoe, however, was only five years old when the Great Plague struck. He based his account on letters from that time, printed testimony, government records, and talks with elderly survivors. He was a fanatical fact finder. Nobody left a finer account of life in plague-ravaged London.[13]

Defoe's narrator describes how people suddenly fell dead in the streets and how the great city was "quite abandoned to despair" and "all in tears." To escape infection, the wealthy fled to the countryside, hoping it would not follow them. The common people often locked themselves in their homes and painted red crosses on the doors, with prayers begging the Lord to take pity on the inhabitants. No matter; the plague killed them anyhow. "Dead carts" made their daily rounds, each led by a man on foot ringing a bell and crying, "Bring out your dead." However, many could not get a decent funeral because "coffins were not to be had for the prodigious numbers that fell in such a calamity as this."[14]

Physicians were baffled. To avoid infection, some advised inhaling the fumes of camphor and vinegar and making "a very strong smoke" by burning "pitch, brimstone or gunpowder." When these measures failed, quacks, crooks, and phonies peddled charms, pills, and potions. These "remedies" went by such names as "Infallible preventive pills against the plague," "Neverfailing preservatives against infections," "universal remedy for the plague," and "royal antidote against all kinds

An illustration of a plague doctor. Flowers and incense kept in the "beak" relieved wearers of the stench of death. (c. 1656)

of infection." Some quacks offered printed copies of magical formulas they said would, when recited with sincerity, prevent or cure plague. One formula was printed in the shape of an inverted triangle. It went like this:

ABRACADABRA
ABRACADABR
ABRACADAB
ABARACAD
ABRACA
ABRAC
ABRA
ABR
AB
A

The 1665 plague peaked in August and September, when more than 7,000 Londoners died each week. In all, it claimed 100,000 lives, a quarter of the English capital's population.[15]

Bubonic plague died out nearly everywhere in Europe after 1665, but it still exists in Asia and occurs elsewhere, though outbreaks are not as severe as in past centuries. San Francisco, the leading seaport on the U.S. Pacific coast, had a minor outbreak in the early 1900s. Today, in the United States, plague infects not only rats but also squirrels, chipmunks,

prairie dogs, rabbits, and skunks. From ten to twenty people, mostly campers and hunters in the western states, contract the disease each year, and about one in seven dies. In August 2015, plague sickened a boy who visited Yosemite National Park in California and a visitor to Wyoming's Yellowstone National Park. Both survived. Nowadays, if the infection is caught in time, various drugs can cure it. Health officials advise park visitors not to feed wild animals of any kind, or touch sick or dead ones and to use insect repellent.[16]

THE RISE OF SCIENTIFIC MEDICINE

By the time the plague ended in London, Europeans were beginning to question long-held ideas about the natural world. For centuries, the educated had believed such knowledge came only from the writings of the Greek philosopher Aristotle and other ancient "authorities," whose works set the standards for judging every medical idea. Supposedly, any explanation that differed from theirs could not be true. This assumption changed in the mid-1600s.

Advanced thinkers believed that

observation, experimentation, and reason counted more than printed words in old books. The Italian Galileo Galilei (1564–1642) showed that the sun is the center of the solar system and that planet Earth revolves around this star, not the other way around. Another researcher, the Englishman Sir Isaac Newton (1642–1727), demonstrated how an invisible force called gravity attracts every particle of matter in the universe according to precise mathematical formulas. In this way, the sun's gravitational pull holds the planets in their orbits, just as Earth's gravity draws snowflakes to the ground. Without gravity, the universe would fly apart in chaos.

Traditional ideas about disease also came into question. The terms *doctor* and *physician* once meant a person whose knowledge came from ancient masters like Hippocrates, the "Father of Medicine," and Galen, both Greek. For over a thousand years, the writings of Hippocrates and Galen were sacred to the medical profession, taught in every university. Sickness, they claimed, had two causes. In the first case, it resulted from having too much of a

An etching of Hippocrates, often considered the "Father of Medicine." (1584)

certain "humor," or bodily fluid: blood, phlegm, yellow bile, or black bile. When a person fell ill, it was because he or she had become too hot, too cold, too moist, or too dry. The favored treatment was bleeding—cutting into a vein to reduce the amount of the "excess" humor. For example, doctors bled George Washington four times for a bad cold, taking a total of ninety-six ounces, well over half the blood in his body, and hastening his death. Another treatment intended to restore the balance of bodily fluids was purging: massive vomiting. The second cause of sickness was believed to be "miasmas," poisonous vapors rising from rotting matter in the soil. To clear away "bad air," physicians advised building bonfires in the streets, beating drums, ringing church bells, and firing cannons.

These ideas gradually gave way as a host of discoveries laid the groundwork for scientific medicine. In 1663, Robert Hooke (1635–1703), an English chemist, saw tiny box-like compartments, which he called "cells," in a piece of cork he was examining under a crude microscope. He soon found that his own hair and skin also contained cells; thus, he concluded, cells are the basic structure of all life-forms.

Antony van Leeuwenhoek, considered the world's first microbiologist, in a painting by Jan Verkolje. (1673)

Meanwhile, Antony van Leeuwenhoek (1632–1723), a Dutch merchant with a passion for science, built better microscopes than had ever existed. Instantly, another world, swarming with life, opened before his eyes. In 1683, the Dutchman observed "animalcules," or what we call microorganisms, tiny life-forms invisible to the naked eye. After viewing a drop of dirty canal water for the first time, he wrote about seeing "with great wonder . . . many very little living animalcules, very prettily a-moving. The biggest sort . . . had a very strong and swift motion, and shot . . . like a pike does through water. The second sort . . . oft spun around like a top." These were the simplest forms of animal life, single-celled creatures such as amoebas. Though Leeuwenhoek was the first human to see bacteria, he did not realize they could cause disease.[17]

The discovery of animalcules did, however, lead the Dutchman to question the theory of *spontaneous generation*. This theory held that simple life-forms—worms, maggots, fleas, lice—arose from nonliving matter such as dust, mud, or dead flesh. Though Leeuwenhoek's studies showed that these creatures emerged from eggs, he failed to convince the scientific community of his day. Acceptance would have to wait until the nineteenth century.

Louis Pasteur (1822–1895), a French chemist and researcher, settled the question of spontaneous generation. During the 1860s, in a series of careful experiments, he proved that new life can arise only from existing life, not from dirt or other lifeless matter. Equally important, Pasteur championed *germ theory,* the idea that microorganisms cause diseases. "The microbe causes the illness," he declared. "Look for the microbe and you'll understand the illness." A German physician, Robert Koch (1843–1910), later found that specific types of microbes cause specific infectious diseases. The discoveries of Pasteur and Koch were like golden keys unlocking nature's secrets. They showed that diseases were not sent as punishment from on high or caused by magic, witchcraft, or the devil. Instead, diseases had natural causes, and the human mind could understand them, control them, and conquer them.[18]

Scientists developed vaccines to

Louis Pasteur, a French chemist and microbiologist renowned for his discoveries of the principles of vaccination, microbial fermentation, and pasteurization, a process that carries his name, in a painting by Albert Edelfelt. (1885)

fight age-old killers. Edward Jenner (1749–1823), an English country doctor, had already used a vaccine to prevent smallpox. Nicknamed the "Speckled Monster," this disease killed its victims outright or left survivors with faces disfigured by deep scars. While making his rounds, Jenner paid special attention to milkmaids, who worked with cows. He noticed that women who got cowpox, a related though nonfatal disease, seemed immune to smallpox. To test his theory, in 1796 Jenner "vaccinated" (from *vacca,* Latin for "cow") a local boy, eight years old— that is, he scratched pus from cowpox sores into the boy's arm. Sure enough, the child developed a low fever but not the fatal or disfiguring smallpox. Several weeks later, to check his theory, Jenner scraped pus from actual smallpox sores into the boy's arm. Again, a low fever but no disease: the boy was immune.[19]

Nineteenth-century scientists followed Jenner's lead. Between 1879 and 1897, vaccines against cholera, anthrax, rabies, typhoid fever, yellow fever, diphtheria, and bubonic plague became available in Europe and America. But neither Jenner nor anyone else understood how vaccines worked. We will learn the answer in another chapter.

Surgery also advanced from the mid-1800s onward. Until then, patients dreaded the pain inevitable in any operation. To keep a person from squirming when the surgeon cut, leather straps and strong men held him or her down. The surgeon

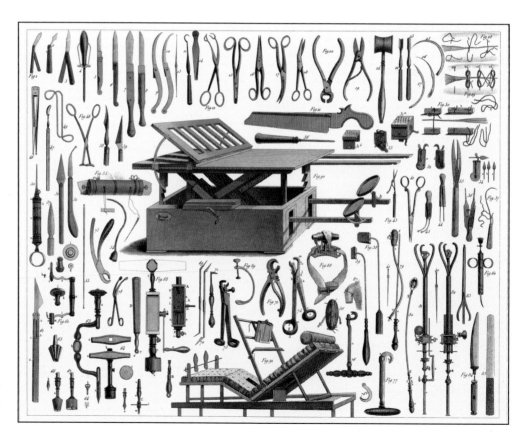

Nineteenth-century surgical tools.

had to be tough-minded, someone who had schooled himself to work quickly and ignore screams. Novelist Fanny Burney left a chilling account of her breast operation in 1810: "When the dreadful steel was plunged into the breast, I began a scream that lasted . . . during the whole time of the incision—& I almost marvel that it rings not in my Ears still! So excruciating was the agony." Burney was lucky; she survived. Many others died of shock, which occurs when the blood fails to circulate properly in the body.[20]

Surgery changed dramatically in the 1840s, as ingenious dentists and physicians began to use anesthetics, drugs that put patients into a deep sleep, making them insensitive to pain. The first such drug, nitrous oxide, or "laughing gas," made patients giddy after inhaling it, then unconscious for a short time—just enough to pull a tooth. Inhaling the fumes of ether and chloroform put them out for longer periods. This allowed for more complicated procedures on parts of the body surgeons had seldom operated on with success: the abdomen, chest, and brain.

Anesthesia also became a blessing to women in childbirth. In 1853, for example, England's Queen Victoria gave birth while under chloroform. "The effect was soothing, quieting & delightful beyond measure," Her Majesty told her diary.[21]

Anesthetics, however, did nothing to prevent infection, the chief cause of surgical deaths. Before Pasteur's germ theory changed medical thinking, surgery and infection were synonymous. Surgical masks, gowns, and gloves did not exist until the early 1900s. Surgeons wore their street clothes, and only washed their hands *after* operating.

In 1918, William W. Keen (1837–1932), America's first brain surgeon, recalled how, as a young doctor, he operated on wounded Union army soldiers during the Civil War:

We surgeons in 1861–65 [were] utterly unaware of bacteria and their dangers. . . . May *le bon Dieu* [the good God] forgive us our sins of ignorance. We operated in old blood-stained and often pus-stained coats, veterans of a hundred fights.

Before the 1840s, amputations were conducted without anesthesia. (Date unknown)

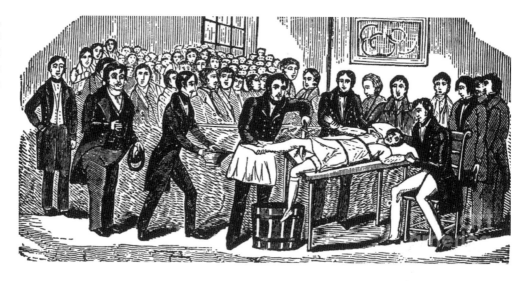

We operated with . . . undisinfected hands. We used undisinfected instruments from undisinfected plush-lined cases, and still worse, used marine sponges which had been used in prior pus cases and had been washed only in tap water. If a sponge or an instrument fell to the floor, it was washed and squeezed in a basin of tap water and used as if it were clean. . . . The silk with which we sewed up all wounds was undisinfected. If there was any difficulty in threading the needle we moistened it with (as we now know) bacteria-laden saliva, and rolled it between bacteria-infected fingers. We dressed the wounds with clean but undisinfected sheets, shirts, tablecloths, or other old soft linen rescued from the family ragbag. We had no sterilized gauze dressing, no gauze sponges. . . . Death was peering over the shoulder of the surgeon, watching for his victim.[22]

No wonder patients routinely developed lethal infections after "successful" operations. Nor should we be surprised that when President Abraham Lincoln lay dying with a bullet in his head, doctors probed for it in the usual way. One by one, they poked their fingers into the wound—unwashed fingers with dirt caked under the nails.

Humanity owes the English surgeon Joseph Lister (1827–1912) a huge debt of gratitude. Inspired by Pasteur's germ theory of disease, Lister demanded absolute cleanliness in the operating room. At first, he ordered that carbolic acid, made from coal tar, be sprayed to kill airborne bacteria. He soon realized that the surgeon's hands and instruments swarmed with unseen killers, so he insisted those be sprayed, too. Equally important, he urged that the moment a surgeon took a scalpel to a patient, antiseptics be used to sterilize the wound. "Listerism" became the rage, the success of his methods leading to their adoption by hospitals throughout the Western world. As a result, deaths from infections following surgery fell from 45 to 15 percent. Today, they are near zero.

Meanwhile, specialized instruments became available to physicians. The stethoscope enabled them to detect abnormalities in the heart and lungs by listening to the sounds these organs produced. The clinical thermometer measured changes in body temperature, while the hypodermic syringe injected medicine into the bloodstream through a hol-

One of René Laennec's early stethoscopes. Laennec invented the instrument in 1816.

low needle. X-rays, discovered by the German physicist Wilhelm Roentgen in 1895, allowed physicians to look into patients' bodies without having to cut them open.

Aspirin, developed in 1897, reduced fever, becoming the world's most widely used medicine. Vitamins were discovered in 1906, and the first successful human blood transfusion took place the following year. Milk was "pasteurized," heated to kill bacteria. Governments, too, acted upon the germ theory, promoting better sanitation, pest control, and water purification. Devices that we in the West now take for granted—like flush toilets, vacuum cleaners, refrigerators, and window screens—began to keep homes cleaner and food fresh. Fashions changed. To avoid bacteria, men shaved their beards and women shortened their dresses so they wouldn't sweep along the foul streets. Newly created public health services checked age-old killers. Deaths from tuberculosis, for example, which mainly affects the lungs, fell from around one in four Americans in 1800 to one in ten by the start of the twentieth century.[23]

Despite its victories, scientific medicine had its opponents. Many devout Christians rejected any teaching that conflicted with the literal text of the Bible. For them, as for people during the Black Death, disease was "a judgment of God on the sins of the people." Edward Jenner's discovery of vaccination drew harsh criticism from the pulpit. Clergymen denounced the doctor for hav-

ing put himself above God. Only the Almighty, they said, sends illness and only the Almighty cures it. Vaccination, critics charged, was "a diabolical operation," and its inventor was "flying in the face of Providence." Anti-vaccination societies sprang up on both sides of the Atlantic. In Boston, clergymen railed against vaccination's "bidding defiance to Heaven itself, even to the will of God." Cartoonists drew pictures of skeletons vaccinating babies and of snakes labeled VACCINATION hissing at babies and their terrified mothers.[24]

Some critics insisted that Satan was the true father of anesthesia. Its development, they warned, was part of his unholy plan to turn humanity away from God. The pains of childbirth, they argued, were divine punishment for Adam and Eve's disobedience in the Garden of Eden. Pain, therefore, was humanity's lot, an inevitable aspect of divine justice.

And as late as the 1870s, several prominent physicians challenged the germ theory of disease. The most famous of these was Samuel D. Gross of Philadelphia. Known as "America's Surgeon" and the "Emperor of American Surgery," Gross

A cartoon from a December 1894 anti-vaccination publication.

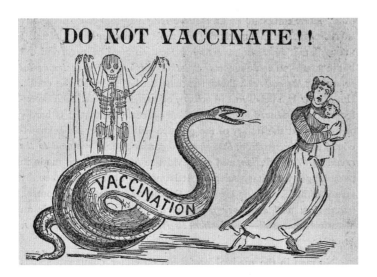

denounced Listerism as quackery. "The demonstration of disease producing germs," he thundered, "is wanting and I have never found any appreciable benefits from the use of antiseptic dressings."[25]

Artist Thomas Eakins immortalized the doctor in *The Gross Clinic* (1875), often called America's greatest painting. Eakins depicts an operation on a patient's infected leg bone. Gross's assistants administer anesthesia and hold the wound open with curved steel tools. Like them, Gross is unmasked, ungloved, and wearing street clothes. He has stepped back, a bloody scalpel in his bloody hand, to lecture students. These are seated in an open gallery overlooking the operating table, breathing their germs toward the gaping wound. Sometimes the eminent surgeon sharpened his scalpel on the sole of his boot, a practice not shown in the painting.[26]

Medicine's Samuel Grosses, however, were a dying breed. Scientific medicine's best arguments were beyond dispute: it saved lives and alleviated suffering. By 1900, for the first time since cities came into existence, European and American cities recorded more births than deaths. We

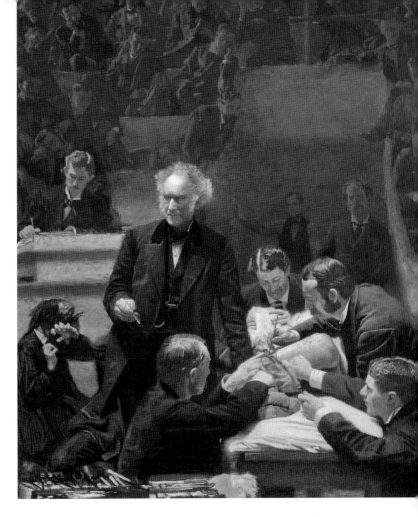

The Gross Clinic by Thomas Eakins, regarded as one of the finest American paintings. (1875)

get a hint of what this meant from a simple name change. People used to call the house parlor the "laying-out room," because dead family members lay there in their coffins awaiting burial. The parlor now became the "living room," where the family spent its leisure time and entertained guests.[27]

The medical profession had reason for pride in itself and optimism about the future. In one century, it had learned more about disease than in all of human history. The physician had come into his own. (We say "his" because, thus far, few women had become medical doctors.) No longer was he a "quack" or a "sawbones" who hacked off limbs for a living. He was a new kind of priest, a holy man in a white coat, the symbol of purity and expertise. The *Medical Times and Hospital Gazette,* an English journal, expressed this view in glowing terms. "The good physician is prepared to meet any emergency that may arise," it stated. "He is a 'friend in need,' a tower of strength in the sick room. He is the man upon whom the people have learned to depend when sickness occurs and Death hovers over their dwelling."[28]

The American physician, according to Dr. Victor C. Vaughan, had become a "co-worker with the Creator." *Outlook,* a popular American magazine, declared the medical profession God's instrument, a sacred thing, because "it is not 'God's will' that children should die of diphtheria or young men be destroyed in the flower of their manhood by typhoid fever." The sky was the limit. "Public health is purchasable," proclaimed a publication of New York City's Department of Health. "Within natural limitations a community can determine its own death-rate." A prominent physician announced, "No one fears a repetition of the ghastly scenes of the Black Death in the fourteenth century." Obviously, the conquest of disease was just a matter of will, time, knowledge, and money.[29]

Nevertheless, the medical profession had no idea that it was about to face a stunning crisis. Though it had achieved much, it had not reckoned on the perfect storm that seemed to come out of the blue. In 1918, war and influenza joined forces to ignite history's worst-ever health disaster.

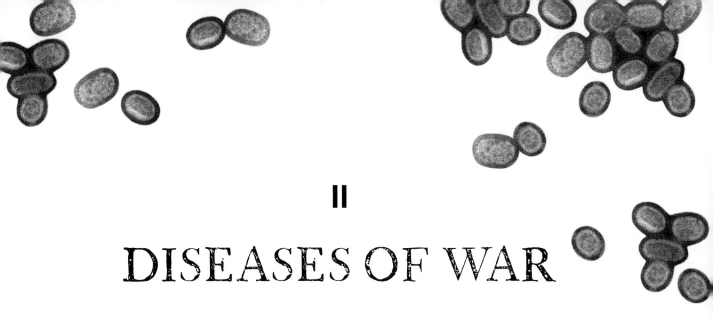

II

DISEASES OF WAR

The history of war has always been a history of epidemics.
—*American Journal of Public Health* editorial, April 1918

BREWING THE PERFECT STORM

Well-clothed, well-fed military officers plan wars in the safety and comfort of headquarters far from future battlefields. Cautious and meticulous, they try to think of every move and circumstance in advance. There is, however, a problem. What former heavyweight champion Mike Tyson once said about boxing also applies to the military: "Everyone has a plan until they get punched in the mouth." Despite officers' best efforts, war plans go awry the moment fighting begins. The reason is simple: the human mind is not omniscient; it cannot foresee everything that can happen. Stupidity, bad information, enemy actions, and dumb luck all play a role in the outcome of battle. Thus, armies, like prizefighters, must quickly adapt to changing conditions or face defeat.

The war that began in July 1914 came as a shock to everyone. Both the Allied and the German high commands had planned their opening moves in minute detail. Optimists, both sides expected a fast-paced war of movement. There would be attacks by masses of soldiers advancing shoulder to shoulder across open fields. By sheer weight of numbers, each side thought, its army would rout the enemy and seize his capital, gaining victory in a blaze of glory. "On to Berlin!" cried Allied troops as they boarded trains for the front; "On to Paris!" shouted German troops. Few expected the war to last beyond Christmas. By the time Santa Claus arrived with his goodies, Daddy would surely be home, safe and sound. As a popular song told the folks in England, "Keep the home fires burning."

Planners, tragically, did not reckon on the effects of the new weapons developed since the 1880s, weapons that would be used for the first time in large-scale combat during the war. On the Western Front, where French, Belgian, and British armies opposed the German advance, machine guns, heavy artillery,

and repeating rifles slaughtered entire units within minutes. On just one day, August 22, 1914, over 27,000 French soldiers died in battle. Afterward, a stunned captain found 300 of them lying in a perfectly straight line. "At the first whistling of bullets, the officers had cried 'Line up!' and all went to death as if on parade," the captain later wrote. Young German soldiers called their horrific losses *Kindermord,* "the children's massacre."[1]

Despite such carnage, the enemies were so evenly matched that neither side could strike a knockout blow. With the chances of surviving in the open so poor, soldiers had to go underground, taking shelter in trenches. By the fall of 1914, opposing trench lines snaked and zigzagged for 550 miles, from the French-Swiss border to the English Channel. The war, a German journalist wrote, had settled into a stalemate, which he called "a worldwide latrine with blood, barbed wire and hate songs."[2]

Latrine was a good word, for it is impossible to exaggerate the misery and squalor of the Western Front. "No Man's Land" lay between the trench lines, a shattered zone, 50

A German trench occupied by British soldiers at Ovillers-la-Boisselle, France, during the Battle of the Somme. The men are from A Company, Eleventh Battalion, the Cheshire Regiment. (July 1916)

to 250 yards wide, of shell craters, wrecked villages, charred forests, and barbed-wire entanglements. Soldiers lived in hollows dug into trench walls or in dugouts, cramped rooms dug as much as 25 feet underground. Emmanuel Bourcier, a French journalist, described dugouts as "really kennels [that stank] of the moldy moisture from the earth itself, of human perspiration, of wet leather and clothing. . . . Everything was dismal, dangerous, frightful." We can understand why the inhabitants called themselves "Death's men"— human beings stuffed into the "sausage machine" of war, existing only to kill until killed themselves.[3]

Every day was an ordeal, "hell with the lid off." In summer, the air shimmered under the blazing sun. In winter, the cold seemed to penetrate the human body's every cell. "We don't think of death," a French soldier wrote his sweetheart. "But it's the cold, the terrible cold! It seems to me at the moment that my blood is full of blocks of ice."[4]

When it rained, as it often did in Belgium and northern France, the front became a swamp of sticking, sucking mud. "The rain drives on," recalled the English painter Paul Nash, "the stinking mud becomes more evilly yellow, the shell-holes fill up with green-white water, the roads . . . are covered with inches of slime, the black dying trees ooze and sweat. . . . It is unspeakable, godless, hopeless."[5]

Trenches became waterlogged, forcing soldiers to stand knee-deep in mud for days. This led to "trench foot," severe swelling that caused the skin on sufferers' feet and legs to

An unidentified sergeant and Henry Basil Ault, the company quartermaster sergeant of the Eleventh Battalion, Lancashire Fusiliers, in a flooded communication trench near Ploegsteert Wood, Belgium. (January 1917)

swell, crack, and peel off in sheets. Worse, for a thousand years farmers had fertilized the fields of Belgium and northern France with manure, their own and that of their animals. Therefore, the tiniest scratch or scrape let in germs and, with them, as an American noted, "an unprecedented riot of infection." The result: "Every wound is infected and with an intensity unknown prior to 1914 either in civilian or military surgery." Blood poisoning set in, and often minor wounds turned fatal for lack of antiseptics. Bacterial infections also led to thousands of leg amputations a week. Amputees might survive. But for the wounded left on the battlefield, the deep mud might as well have been quicksand. Injured men often drowned, pulled under before medics got to them.[6]

The front, wrote the English poet Siegfried Sassoon, was "rotten with dead." Rain and shelling constantly churned up bodies and body parts hastily buried just inches deep. The smell of rot filled the air, particularly during warm weather. There was no escaping it. A French soldier recalled: "We all had on us the stench of dead bodies. The bread we ate, the

German soldiers pick lice out of their undergarments. (c. 1915-1918)

stagnant water we drank, everything we touched had a rotten smell."[7]

Soldiers stank, too. Unable to wash because what little fresh water they had was needed for drinking, they became grungy. French soldiers called themselves *poilu* and Germans *Frontschweinen,* "hairy ones" and "front-line pigs," respectively, referring to their unshaven faces, filth, and evil smell. When large bodies of troops marched through a village, civilians shut their windows to keep out the odor. "Our master is our misery," a Frenchman wrote. Another wrote that they were living "a life so frightfully bestial [that] even pigs are better off!"[8]

Clothing and bodies crawled with lice, tiny insects that inject bacteria with each bite. Female lice were so fertile, said one *poilu,* that a louse born in the morning was a grandmother by evening. Lice carried "trench fever," an infection causing high temperature and putting men out of action for a month, though seldom causing death. Typhus, another lice-borne disease, killed them. Whether a soldier got sick or not, a louse bite caused intense itching, rattling the most hard-bitten veteran. "I never thought a man would be driven to such a state of frenzy by a louse," a rookie noted. The words *lousy* and *crummy*—because lice were the color of toasted bread crumbs—came to mean anything nasty or unpleasant. Whenever possible, soldiers took time out to "read

A typical trench-rat haul. Small dogs helped flush rats into the open. (1916)

their shirts," picking lice out of the seams and crushing them between their fingers.[9]

Then there were the rats "bigger than cats." Grown fat from feasting on the dead, a single pair could produce 880 babies a year. Soldiers dreaded rats as carriers of bubonic plague, and their incessant squeaking rang in men's ears. Squatting over a latrine risked exposing one's backside to their bite. At night, rats scampered among the sleeping men. They nosed into pockets for food or nibbled on ears, lips, and noses. Even worse, the red-eyed demons "would eat a wounded man if he couldn't defend himself." A French patrol once came upon several corpses. "I saw some rats running from under the dead men's greatcoats," a soldier wrote. "My heart pounded as we edged toward one of the bodies. . . . The man displayed a grimacing face, stripped of flesh; his skull bare, the eyes devoured, and from the yawning mouth leapt a rat." Rats liked to start with the eyes, eventually reducing the body to a skeleton. Soldiers loathed them, staging "ratting hunts" with pistols, shovels, and clubs.[10]

Front-line troops lived under continual stress. Rats and lice, fear and noise, made restful sleep impossible. "I felt I would barter my soul for a few hours of uninterrupted slumber," a soldier noted. "What kills," said another, "is the absence of sleep." Lack of sleep left men confused, listless—and careless.[11]

To survive, a soldier had to consider his every movement, since enemy snipers shot anyone who showed himself for even an instant. Moreover, a new weapon, the airplane, appeared in large numbers. In 1903, two bicycle repairers from Ohio, Orville and Wilbur Wright, had built the first successful heavier-than-air flying machine. Idealists, the Wright brothers believed aviation would abolish war. "[It] will prevent war," Orville declared, "by making it too expensive, too slow, too difficult, too long drawn out." They could not have been more wrong. By 1915, "winged death" swooped over enemy trenches without warning, dropping bombs and spraying machine-gun bullets.[12]

However, nothing compared to attacking across No Man's Land. Every attack began with an artillery bombardment to weaken and disorient the defenders. Heavy guns massed behind the trench lines fired day and night, often for a week, pausing only to let the overheated gun barrels cool. Sound waves struck the gunners' ears like fists, making them ring, even causing lifelong deafness.

Bombardments were an ordeal

Soldiers of an Australian Fourth Division field artillery brigade on a duckboard track passing through Château Wood, near Hooge, Belgium. (1917)

for the assault troops huddled in their trenches, awaiting the order to advance. "The sound waves were going over your head all the time, like a tuning fork being struck on your steel helmet," a British soldier wrote. "A terrible sound—ping, ping, ping, ping—this terrible vibration day and night and this noise in your head . . . went right through you. You couldn't get away from it. It went right down into your nerves." Sometimes, when shells fell short, men died from "friendly fire"—that is, an attack coming from one's own side. No fewer than 75,000 French troops were killed or wounded by their own artillery.[13]

Soldiers on the bombardment's receiving end could only hunker down and pray under "a tornado of bursting shells." A young German soldier named Adolf Hitler was traumatized by what he called "the everlasting artillery fire." Years later, as Germany's dictator, he could go on for five minutes at a time with imitations of the different sounds the shells made as they flew through the air. But a shell had no mind; it exploded harmlessly or among those whose bad luck it was to be at the wrong

place at the wrong time. The ground shook. Geysers of earth leaped into the air. Sharp metal splinters zinged and whooshed in all directions. The splinters decapitated men, sliced them in half, or simply passed them by. Explosions crippled men or blew them to bits; many soldiers vanished in a red spray. Trenches and dugouts caved in, burying everyone.[14]

Grown men became children again, crying, "Mommy," *"Maman,"* and *"Mutti."* They cringed, whimpering like scared puppies, "Oh, God, make it stop!" Many cracked up from "shell shock," a mental disorder brought on by intense, prolonged fear. An English doctor described how men in "the flower and vigor of youth" became "doddering palsied wrecks, quivering at a sound, dreading the visions of the night." Many recovered with rest in a safe place; many others remained mental wrecks.[15]

When the bombardment lifted, the attacking infantry charged into No Man's Land. By then, the defenders had emerged from cover and were ready to receive them. Answering artillery, machine-gun, and rifle fire slaughtered the oncoming troops.

Heavy artillery fire from the British Royal Tank Regiment. (c. 1917)

Few attacks gained ground, much less overran the enemy trenches. Attackers suffered frightful losses. For example, on July 1, 1916, the first day of the Battle of the Somme, the British took nearly 60,000 casualties, of whom 19,000 lost their lives. The battle raged until November, costing both sides over a million casualties. Yet the trench lines held firm.[16]

In 1915, the Germans used poison gas for the first time, and the Allies answered in kind. This "breath from the depths of hell," as a French writer called poison gas, began the age of what we call weapons of mass destruction (WMD). The gases were released from artillery shells or steel canisters planted in the ground downwind from the enemy. The most-used types, chlorine and mustard gas, looked and smelled different. Chlorine gas formed a light green haze and smelled like strong laundry bleach. Mustard gas was a dark yellow vapor that smelled like mustard, onion, or garlic.[17]

Both types of gas blinded soldiers, burned their flesh, and choked them. The "lucky" ones went quickly, but most suffered for several days. A journalist described what he saw in the gas ward of a French field hospital: "As you walked down the aisle by the rows of cots, you could see how the different ones were suffering.

TOP: A soldier caught in a gas attack without his mask. (c. 1915-1918)

BOTTOM: A donkey in an ill-fitting gas mask. Many animals succumbed to the effects of poison gas because of a lack of specialized equipment. (Date unknown)

The gas mask, a clumsy rubber-and-canvas device containing charcoal to purify the air a soldier breathed, was the only shield against the deadly vapors. Special masks also provided protection for war dogs, horses, and donkeys, which suffered as badly as humans. Poison gas had only one thing in its favor: it reduced the rat population for a day or two.

Still the war dragged on.

AMERICA GOES TO WAR

By 1917, it was clear that victory would have little to do with brilliant generalship or raw courage. It would go to the side best able to keep stuffing the most men into the "sausage machine" until enemy resistance broke. Allied leaders counted on the United States to tilt the balance in their favor. Repeatedly, they urged President Woodrow Wilson to make an all-out effort to send an army as quickly as possible. The AEF, short for American Expeditionary Force, would be the United States' first mass army to fight overseas.

America mobilized for war. In the past, when nations fought, military action had little direct impact on civilians unless they had the bad

Some of them in places where their eyes were, were just large bleeding scabs; others their mouths were just one mass of sores; others had their hands up, and there were terrible burns beneath their arms, where the gas had attacked the moisture there."[18]

luck to live in a battle zone. Usually, civilians went about their business as if the fighting were raging on a distant planet. This war was different. It began the era of total war, which could be waged only by harnessing the entire society for the effort. The "home front" became as vital as the fighting front. In a sense, civilians became soldiers, working in factories and on the land to produce whatever the fighters needed.

Within weeks of declaring war on Germany, the United States began to marshal its resources. By law, scores of federal boards, bureaus, offices, and agencies reshaped the peacetime economy to meet wartime needs. They decided what goods factories could manufacture, what materials they could use, and what their owners could charge. Railroads had to give priority to moving troops, weapons, and raw materials. Ocean liners became troopships. Labor unions gave no-strike pledges for the duration of the war; strikers could be drafted, fined, or given long prison terms. The government's main task, however, was to form the AEF, train it, and send it safely across the Atlantic Ocean. But none of this could happen without safeguarding the soldiers' health.

The U.S. War Department recruited a top-notch medical team to advise it on needed health measures and design programs to make them work. The surgeon general of the army, William Crawford Gorgas (1854–1920), had discovered how to control malaria and yellow fever by destroying the mosquitoes that carried the disease-causing parasites and viruses. Victor C. Vaughan (1851–1929) was dean of the medical school at the University of Michigan. Rufus Cole (1872–1966) served as director of the Rockefeller University Hospital in New York City. Simon Flexner

General William Crawford Gorgas. (Date unknown)

Dr. Victor C. Vaughan. (Date unknown)

(1863–1946) headed the Rockefeller Institute for Medical Research. William H. Welch (1850–1934), of the Johns Hopkins University School of Medicine in Baltimore, was the dean of American medicine. The soft-spoken, gray-bearded Welch was past president of the American Medical Association, the National Academy of Science, and the American Association for the Advancement of Science.

These men knew medical history. Battle, horrible as it was, had always killed fewer soldiers than had disease. War and disease were opposite sides of the same lethal coin. Armies were ideal vehicles for crowd diseases; their gathering inevitably brought serious health problems. Few civilians, even in developed Western countries, traveled long distances, and limited contact among them usually checked the spread of infectious diseases. In wartime, however, large bodies of men were constantly on the move. Recruits from different disease environments—from urban slums, rural villages, and isolated farms—crowded into training camps. They slept close to each other, ate together, showered together, and breathed the same air. Combat made matters worse because hardship, stress, fatigue, exposure, and poor hygiene weakened resistance to infectious diseases.

Such diseases were part of the American military experience. We have few statistics about the French and Indian War (1754–1763), but private letters and official reports mention the ravages of smallpox and typhoid fever. During the American War of Independence (1775–1783), George Washington's battered army camped at Valley Forge, Pennsylvania, in the winter of 1777–1778. Besides the diseases already mentioned, dysentery—uncontrollable diarrhea caused by bacterial infection—was a common killer. "How're your bowels?" soldiers asked, half in jest.[19]

During the Civil War (1861–1865), four Union army soldiers died of sickness for every one killed in battle, and two out of three deaths in the Confederate army resulted from infectious diseases. On each side, measles was the leading killer of soldiers. Measles usually infects children, causing coughing, a rash, and other discomfort, but seldom death. When, however, the disease strikes adults, it is merciless. An official Union army report described its impact on military operations: "Frequently from one-third to one-half of the effective strength [of a regiment] was attacked [by measles]. . . . No part of the army escaped." The chilling conclusion: "For all troops, there was a much greater chance of dying from disease than in the heat of battle." Civil War soldiers were five times as likely to die of an infectious disease as civilians who stayed home.[20]

In 1917, the War Department's star medical team knew what to expect. Proud of their expertise and the status of the medical profession, they resolved that infectious diseases would not decimate the AEF. No

shrinking violet, Dr. Vaughan reeled off facts with the calm authority of a medical school dean. "The mobilization of an army is a medical as well as a military problem," he warned army brass. "[Making] raw, untrained men . . . into effective soldiers [has] always been accompanied by marked increase in morbidity [sickness] and mortality." Crowd diseases could turn training camps into "drag-nets" for infections.[21]

Science had already helped bring under control some of the diseases that had devastated armies in the past. By 1918, the U.S. army was vaccinating recruits against smallpox, cholera, typhoid fever, and anthrax. Vaughan suggested other sensible measures: more Medical Corps doctors, more hospitals, more nutritious food, less crowding in barracks, better sanitation. The army should assemble newly drafted recruits into groups of not more than thirty near their homes. There they would be examined, vaccinated, bathed, scrubbed, issued clean uniforms, and isolated for two weeks, long enough for symptoms of any disease they might have to show up.[22]

Officers responsible for training

U.S. soldiers line up to
receive typhoid fever
vaccinations during
World War I. (1917)

the AEF had different concerns. Armies, they declared, existed to win wars. "The purpose of mobilization," Vaughan and his colleagues were told, "is to convert civilians into trained soldiers as quickly as possible and not to make a demonstration in preventive medicine." Translation: You may give any advice you wish, but remember that the military has a job to do, and that job comes first.[23]

A sentence in the army's official medical manual fairly leaped off the page. It said that the prime concern of military physicians was the "preservation of the strength of the Army in the field." It followed, as one officer put it, that "from a cold military standpoint the care of the well and strong is more important than the care of the ill and feeble." War is a taskmaster; it demands hard, often cruel, choices. Nothing could be worse than losing a war; such a loss could threaten the nation's very existence. So "a patient's interests" had to yield to "the stern activities of war."[24]

Professional medical judgment,

therefore, was at odds with the necessities of waging war. In peacetime, the physician's duty was to preserve the health of any *individual* who needed help. But in the war's big picture, an individual doughboy's life counted for little; his loss was merely "wastage," an inevitable cost of carrying out a mission. Similarly, the physician was bound not only by professional standards but also by the patriotic duty to prepare recruits to fight for "the greater good," as defined by a democratically elected government. Frustrating as these facts were, a different challenge soon revealed a critical gap in physicians' knowledge: they knew nothing about viruses.[25]

OF BACTERIA AND VIRUSES

In 1918, when physicians used the term *virus,* derived from the Latin for "a poisonous force," they meant toxins (poisons) given off by bacteria. No less an authority than Sir William Osler (1849–1919), the leading English physician of the day, spoke of the "virus of anthrax," a bacterial disease attacking plant-eating animals. Osler had no idea that viruses are separate entities, unlike bacteria in every way. To understand the difference, we must base our discussion on research done in the decades after World War I.[26]

Physicians already knew a lot about how bacteria looked and behaved. Bacteria are single-celled organisms. We call them organisms because they do everything necessary for life. They take in and digest food, use energy to grow and develop, and eliminate waste. Bacteria reproduce by growing to twice their normal size and then splitting into two "daughter" cells, each exact copies of the "parent." Bacteria can divide about once every twenty minutes. At that rate, a single bacterium may produce four sextillion (the number 4 followed by twenty-one zeros) copies of itself.[27]

All living cells, from the single cell of a bacterium to the billions of cells that make up a human being, contain strands of a material called *deoxyribonucleic acid*—DNA for short. Joined in a double helix, these strands resemble a spiral staircase. DNA is the chemical instruction manual for how living organisms look and function.

The double-stranded helix of DNA.

Segments of DNA strands called *genes* control heredity, the passing of physical qualities from parent to offspring.

Bacteria are the oldest known life-forms. Microscopic fossils reveal they have been around for at least 3.5 billion years. Fossils also show that they attacked *Tyrannosaurus rex,* a huge flesh-eating dinosaur that roamed the earth 65 million years ago. Scientists have found living bacteria in every environment: water, soil, clouds, hot springs, volcanic vents, Arctic ice, and the oceans' depths. What is more, bacteria live on and in the human body: our skin, hair, nose, mouth, teeth, eyelids, stomach, intes-

tines, and lungs. Amazingly, we have ten times as many bacterial cells in our bodies as human cells. As biologist Thomas Borody jokingly put it, "We are 10 percent human, 90 percent poo."[28]

Bacteria cause diseases such as bubonic plague, typhoid fever, typhus, tuberculosis, cholera, diphtheria, and whooping cough. They enter our bodies with the air we inhale, in the water we drink and the food we eat, through breaks in our skin, during sexual activity. However, less than 1 percent of the thousands of known types of bacteria make us sick. Most are usually harmless and often helpful. Life could not exist on Earth without these tiniest of organisms. Bacteria produce about half the oxygen in our planet's atmosphere. Some types purify water in sewage-treatment plants; some break down oil spills. Still others act as nature's waste-disposal crews, dissolving dead animals and plants. Many life-forms need the chemicals bacteria leave behind to survive. Bacteria, too, help our bodies digest food and produce vitamins K and B_{12}, both essential to health.[29]

Viruses are much simpler things.

We call them "things" because they are merely bundles of genetic material enclosed in a protein envelope called a capsule. Their genes are either double-stranded DNA or single strands of *ribonucleic acid*—RNA for short. Nobel Prize–winning biologist Peter Medawar defined the virus as "a piece of bad news wrapped up in protein." Viruses *are* bad news. Throughout the ages, they have caused dreadful diseases: measles, mumps, polio, chicken pox, smallpox, hepatitis, rabies, Ebola, AIDS, and influenza, to name a few.[30]

Virologists—scientists who study viruses—have identified and described about 5,000 types, though they suspect a million others may exist. Viruses are found wherever there are living cells to invade. Their numbers are astounding, more than all earthly creatures combined. Science writer Carl Zimmer estimates there are about a nonillion (the number 1 followed by thirty zeros) viruses in the oceans alone. Were you to put all of them on a scale, they would equal the weight of seventy-five million blue whales, the largest living creatures.[31]

Yet viruses are tiny, about 1/10,000th of a millimeter; a billion could fit onto the head of a pin. Viruses can pass through the finest filters and are invisible under ordinary microscopes. Many virologists say viruses exist on the edge of life, somewhere between a living organism and a pure chemical. They do not consider them to be alive, because viruses have no working parts—unlike bacteria, they can do nothing on their own.

For a virus to harm humans, six things need to happen: (1) The virus must emerge from the animal that shelters its kind. (2) It must be spread easily by its human host—through coughing, sneezing, touching, kissing, or sexual activity. (3) It must enter human cells quickly, because it cannot exist for long outside its host. (4) Once inside a host, it needs to evade a savage hunter, the human immune system. (5) It has to hijack living cells, forcing them to make more of its own kind. (6) The next generation of the virus must spread from person to person; if it cannot, its type will disappear.

Viruses seem to exist for one purpose only: to reproduce. Nevertheless, they cannot divide like bacteria or have sex like animals. Yet viruses are fussy; different types zero in on specific types of cells but not on other types. A target cell may be a bacterium of a certain kind, or the target cell may be one of the specialized cells that make up the tissues and organs of complex creatures like ourselves.

Let's say a certain type of virus targets epithelial cells—tissue that lines the skin, mouth, intestines, etc. After finding its prey, the virus attaches itself to the cell wall, gradually forcing its way inside. Once inside, the virus sheds its protein envelope and releases its DNA or RNA genes (it cannot have both) into the nucleus, which is the cell's command-and-control center. As if ordering the nucleus, "Stop what you are doing and obey me!" the invading genes reprogram the cell's genes to make copies of the virus. The cell has no choice; it must become the invader's slave. Now unable to tend to its own needs, the cell can only manufacture copies of the virus. Before long, the cell fills with "newborn" viruses until it can hold no more. At that point, the viruses burst through the wall, killing the weakened cell, and go on to in-

fect nearby cells of the same kind. As the infection spreads, either the host creature dies or its immune system fights off the infection. No other outcome is possible.

Our immune system ranks high among Mother Nature's marvels. Its job is to distinguish "self" from "nonself"—that is, the body's own cells from the cells of invaders. When a bacterium or a virus enters our body, chemicals called *cytokines* (from Greek words meaning "cell movement") detect the intruder immediately. Saying, in effect, "You are not of me," the chemicals send out signals to trigger the body's defenses. The first sign of trouble is fever, the body's way of "baking" intruders to death.

Meanwhile, more aid rushes to the infected site. Key aid givers are two types of white blood cells known as *leukocytes*. The first type, called *phagocytes,* surrounds intruders and gobbles them up. The second type, called *lymphocytes,* consists of B cells and T cells. Both types patrol the body, always ready for action. B cells make *antibodies,* chemicals that destroy intruders or neutralize the toxins they produce. T cells have more to do. Some destroy the body's own infected cells. Others serve as "memory cells," allowing the immune system to respond quickly to a later invasion by the same or a similar intruder. This is the principle of vaccination: memory cells recognize past intruders, jolting the immune system into action without causing a full-blown infection.

Today, we use the term *virus* for not only natural viruses but also man-made ones. A computer virus is a program that gets into your computer, usually from an infected website or an email attachment. Once inside, it forces your computer to make as many copies of itself as possible, as quickly as possible. This, in turn, uses up all the computer's memory, disabling the machine by making its operating system "freeze"—come to a halt. Viruses can also spread across networks, infecting every computer linked to them. However, various security programs "immunize" computers, preventing viruses from entering, or removing them when they do.

THE DEVIL VIRUS

The influenza virus is unique. Science historian John Barry says it is "among the most perfect" of viruses. What makes it so is its ability to change continually; it *never* stays the same. This cannot be said about other viruses. For instance, the virus that causes polio (infantile paralysis) is very stable, so the same vaccine will give immunity year after year. And if injected before symptoms develop, the rabies vaccine will prevent the disease in a person bitten by any rabid, or "mad," animal.[32]

There are three forms of the influenza virus: Type A, Type B, and Type C. Type C can make humans seriously ill, but it seldom does. Type B is more annoying than dangerous. Type A can become a mass killer. Moreover, humans, whales, horses, pigs, dogs, cats, apes, baboons, walruses, and seals have their own special versions of the Type A virus.[33]

All flu viruses that make humans sick get their start in birds. Wild birds that live in water, especially ducks and geese, are their natural "reservoirs." These viruses live in the birds' intestines. Apparently, over millions of

ANATOMY OF A FLU VIRUS

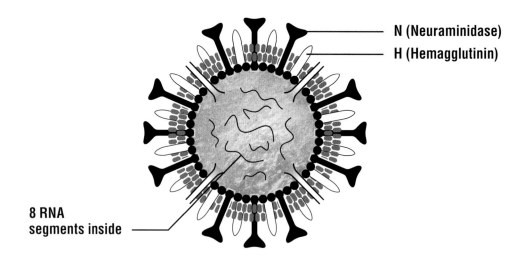

N (Neuraminidase)

H (Hemagglutinin)

8 RNA
segments inside

years, waterbirds and viruses adjusted to this arrangement; they do not harm each other. Humans, however, usually do not get influenza directly from birds. Even when they do, the virus rarely spreads from person to person. For the virus to be able to attack humans, it must first pass through pigs.

Flu viruses may actually drop from the sky. Imagine a flock of wild ducks migrating, flying thousands of miles to winter nesting grounds. As they pass overhead, some drop feces, which happen to land in pigpens. Not surprisingly, bits of the virus-laden

stuff get into the animals' nostrils. The danger lies in some pigs already having two versions of the Type A virus in their bodies: their own and the version from their human handlers. In that case, pig lung cells become "mixing vessels" for bird, pig, and human viral genes.

Mixing works like this: The capsule of the Type A virus is studded with spikes made of two kinds of proteins, known as H and N, shorthand for *hemagglutinin* and *neuraminidase*. Scientists have assigned these proteins numbers based on their appearance. The Type A H1N1 virus was the culprit in the 1918 pandemic. Its H-protein spikes act as grappling hooks to attach the virus to the outer wall of a cell in the throat or lungs before penetrating it. After forcing the host cell to produce more viruses, the new generation's H-protein spikes go into action. Each spike has four propeller-like blades, which slice through the cell's inner wall, freeing the "newborn" viruses. When this happens, between 100,000 and a million viruses literally explode through the cell wall at once.[34]

Influenza viruses have eight genes made of RNA. These differ in a special way from the genes of viruses made of DNA. Each DNA gene has a built-in checking mechanism that scans for copying errors in "newborn" viruses. When these errors are found, a DNA gene can either repair itself or self-destruct. Genes made of RNA lack this self-scanning ability, so the copying errors common in flu genes cannot be fixed or eliminated. To further complicate matters, the genes of flu viruses, unlike the genes of most other viruses, are not aligned to form a single strand. Instead, they come in separate segments. Though

"newborn" viruses still have eight genes, their separate segments allow the genes of birds, humans, and pigs to arrange themselves at random within the same host cell. Virologists call this process *reassortment*. The result of reassortment is a genetic mutation, an aspect that the original virus lacks but its later versions can inherit.

Reassorted Type A bird and pig flu genes enable the virus to move from pig to pig, producing deadly "swine flu." Reassortments of bird and human flu genes allow infection to cross over to people and then from one person to another. Highly contagious, the recombined virus spreads by droplets expelled by coughing and sneezing. A hearty sneeze sends upward of 40,000 virus particles hurtling through the air at a speed of 152 feet per second. Influenza viruses can travel up to twelve feet, and they are so light that they can remain suspended in the air for up to thirty minutes. To become infected, a person has to inhale only one of the suspended viruses. Infection can also come from touching a surface on which a suspended virus has landed.

REASSORTMENT OF A FLU VIRUS IN A PIG HOST

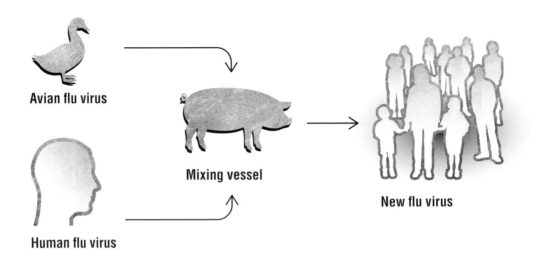

Avian flu virus

Mixing vessel

New flu virus

Human flu virus

This makes influenza an ideal crowd disease.[35]

Most mutations are not extreme. Virologists say viruses *drift*—that is, each generation undergoes a series of small changes. But these "newborn" viruses remain much like the "parent" generation. The similarity is still close enough to allow the human immune system's memory cells to recognize the intruder and mount a defense. Over time, however, mutations accumulate, making it harder to detect later generations of intruders. That is why we need to get an updated version of the flu vaccine every year.

Influenza viruses can also mutate suddenly and dramatically. When this happens, scientists say they *shift,* giving rise to a completely new form of the virus. If this form has a feature that improves its chances to reproduce, such as an enhanced ability to clamp on to a cell wall, it will cause trouble. Because the human immune system has never before encountered such an intruder, it cannot recognize the threat at first, or act to destroy it quickly. What is worse, as a new virus generation passes from person to person, it strengthens with each passage, having gained fresh opportunities for mutation. For example,

SYMPTOMS OF INFLUENZA

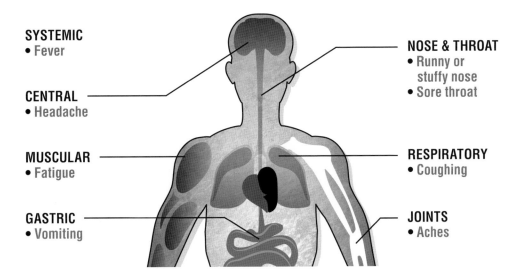

SYSTEMIC
• Fever

CENTRAL
• Headache

MUSCULAR
• Fatigue

GASTRIC
• Vomiting

NOSE & THROAT
• Runny or
  stuffy nose
• Sore throat

RESPIRATORY
• Coughing

JOINTS
• Aches

we now know that the devil virus of 1918 did not start out as a mass killer. But as the infection spread, the virus shifted, becoming deadlier. At the same time, the war acted as an accelerator, creating conditions that allowed the mutated virus to explode into a pandemic that killed tens of millions.

THE FIRST WAVE

Morale in the Allied countries had reached a low point by the fall of 1917. "The war [is] eating into the souls of men," British and French people murmured. A young Londoner told her diary: "[Everywhere]

there is an all-pervading atmosphere of dread."[36]

There was plenty of reason to worry. A four-month campaign in Belgium had cost the British army 250,000 lives and achieved absolutely nothing. In the east, meanwhile, the Russians, who had been suffering crushing defeats, saw revolutionaries topple their government. Almost immediately, they found themselves in a savage civil war. Reds (Communists) and Whites (those loyal to the old monarchy) butchered each other without mercy. Unable to fight a civil war and Germany at the same time, the Reds begged for peace. Germany agreed, and on December 2, 1917, Russia left the war, a major setback for the Allies.

Russia's so-called betrayal allowed Germany to transfer veteran troops to the Western Front, far outnumbering the British and French. By then, America had entered the war and was preparing to send the first trained AEF units overseas. Before those units arrived in strength, the German high command decided to risk everything on an all-out effort to smash the Allies. When an officer asked General Erich Ludendorff (1865–1937), the German commander on the Western Front, what would happen if the offensive failed,

the general fixed him with a cold stare. "Then Germany must perish," Ludendorff snarled. Whether Germany won or lost, he knew the war would end before 1918 was out.[37]

Ludendorff struck on March 21, 1918, the first day of spring. After a massive artillery bombardment, "a storm of steel and fire," his troops broke through the French lines. This was as close as Germany would come to winning the war. Though halted in fierce fighting, Ludendorff held the ground he had taken. From a distance of seventy-five miles, he unleashed "Big Bertha," a giant cannon that hurled 1,800-pound shells into Paris.

The attack did not surprise Allied leaders; aerial photographs had revealed the massive enemy buildup, and they feared the worst. During the first week of March, Georges Clemenceau, the French prime minister, wrote to President Wilson. "A terrible blow is imminent," he said. "Tell your Americans to come quickly." Luckily, by then, every month would see American troops land at French seaports; 84,000 arrived in March alone. They arrived in the nick of time, but they did not travel alone.[38]

No Man's Land: This U.S. soldier, entangled in barbed wire between rival trenches in northern Europe, was one of millions whose lives were claimed by war. (1917)

Historians disagree on where and when the first influenza wave began. Some believe migrating birds flew south from Canadian lakes, as they had done throughout the ages. A duck, most likely, dropped virus-tainted feces into a pig wallow near Fort Riley. Perhaps a farmer carrying a human variety of Type A virus passed it to one of his pigs, and the viruses reassorted and then spread to people. This may explain why recruits at Camp Funston reported sick on March 11, ten days before the German offensive began in France. As troops from Fort Riley moved to other camps for additional training, or to join units bound for France, they brought the infection with them—and eventually across the Atlantic.[39]

Other historians think it a coincidence that the first wave struck Europe just as American troops arrived. They point to Étaples, a village near the seaport of Boulogne, France, as the likely place of origin. Étaples lies on the edge of vast salt marshes, stop-off places favored by flocks of birds on their way to nesting sites in Africa. Nearby lay farms that raised pigs, ducks, geese, and chickens—immense numbers of them. At Étaples, the British army had the largest base it ever built on foreign soil. A railway link served the base's twenty-

Tents at the New Zealand reinforcement camp in Étaples, France. (c. 1914–1918)

four hospitals, placed within easy walking distance of each other. The base also had a prisoner-of-war compound, and camps for fresh troops bound for the front and men returning from the trenches for rest and medical treatment. A historian notes: "Never before or since have so many men and microbes co-existed in the same place for so long."[40]

Étaples was filled with men forced to live in canvas tents or flimsy wooden barracks in all seasons. Impossible to keep clean, the place was damp, depressing, and smelly. Étaples, English poet Wilfred Owen wrote his mother, "seemed neither France nor England, but a kind of paddock where beasts are kept days before the shambles [slaughter]." The troops had a strange look about them, Owen noted. "It was not despair, or terror, it was more terrible than terror, for it was a blindfold look, and without expression, like a dead rabbit's." On any given day, the base held at least 100,000 men, a supercrowd in terms of infectious diseases.[41]

Trench diseases ran riot at Étaples: trench foot, trench fever, dysentery, tetanus, typhus. Bleak hospital wards held victims of gas—poisons, we know today, that cause gene mutations, even cancer. In 1916 and 1917, doctors reported outbreaks of influenza at Étaples. Not only did the infection strike the base, but men returning to the trenches carried the virus to their comrades. Similarly, those on home leave or sent to hospitals in England brought it there, too. In the spring of 1918, the current strain of influenza, or one very much like it, drifted to the point where it erupted into an epidemic.

Wherever the first wave began, at Fort Riley or Étaples, influenza soon washed over the Western Front. The disease appears to have struck the British army first. British generals, sticklers for discipline, would hear no excuses: feverish troops must do their duty! Private Arthur Lapointe recalled how it felt to leave his trench to attack: "As I reach the top, my head swims [and] everything around me whirls. . . . One man can no longer stand erect, and crawls on hands and knees. We leave him behind, with a comrade looking after him." Edouard Froidure, a Belgian soldier, wrote his folks: "For two or three days, I was raving, drained or agitated depending on the moment." Clearly, this was not the familiar seasonal flu.[42]

The virus easily crossed No Man's Land, perhaps brought by Allied prisoners. It played havoc in the German trenches. "Influenza is now epidemic all along the German front," the *New York Times* reported. "Special hospitals are being established in the rear areas dealing solely with this disease."[43]

H1N1 threw a monkey wrench into General Ludendorff's plans, while helping the Allies stall the German advance. "Our army suffered. Influenza was rampant," Ludendorff wrote in his postwar memoirs. "It was a grievous business having to listen every morning to the chiefs of staffs' recital of the number of influenza cases, and their complaints about the weakness of their troops.... [Eventually] the number of influenza cases diminished, although it often left a greater weakness in its wake than the doctors realized." By late summer, the flu had temporarily put half a million German soldiers out of action.[44]

In wartime, casualty rates, even from sickness, are military secrets be-

General Erich Ludendorff. (Date unknown)

cause they may help opponents figure out each other's strength. To keep the extent of the infection secret, the U.S. War Department flat out lied. "The American troops have at no time shown any form of the disease," it announced. Press censorship, moreover, prevented Allied journalists from getting or publishing firsthand information about the extent of the epidemic.[45]

The public learned the truth anyhow. Spain remained neutral throughout the war, refusing to take sides. So it did not have press censorship, and its journalists on both sides of the Western Front knew the score. Besides, viruses do not respect national borders. In May 1918, influenza broke out in Madrid, Spain's capital. Thousands, including King Alfonso XIII, took to their beds. As a result, the Spanish press printed articles about the disease at home and elsewhere in Europe. British and French newspapers reprinted the stories, angering the authorities, who could not plug the leaks. Though the disease did not originate in Spain, people nicknamed it the "Spanish flu," the "Spanish Lady," and the "Plague of the Spanish Lady." Span-iards returned the favor, calling it the "French flu," because they thought it originated in France.[46]

The first wave grew from an epidemic into a pandemic. By July, it had spread worldwide. It surged across oceans and continents, reaching Africa, the Middle East, Asia, the Philippines, Australia, New Zealand, and North and South America. In China, according to an official report, "it swept over the whole country like a tidal wave."[47]

No disease had ever traveled so far, so fast. Bubonic plague had moved

The decomposing body of a German soldier in No Man's Land. (1917)

overland at the speed of a walking person and a horse-drawn wagon and by sea aboard sailing ships battling winds, currents, and tides. The 1918 pandemic was a disease of the Industrial Age, when the world was more closely connected than at any time in the past. Nestled inside infected people, the H1N1 virus traveled hundreds of miles a day aboard automobiles, buses, trucks, trains, and steamships.

Millions suffered during the first wave. Some compared a bout of influenza to a "punch-up," a fistfight with a stronger opponent. An anonymous soldier-poet described his experience this way:

> *When your back is broke and*
> *your eyes are blurred,*
> *And your shin bones knock and*
> *your tongue is furred;*
> *And your tonsils squeak and your*
> *hair gets dry,*
> *And you're doggone sure that*
> *you're going to die,*
> *But you're skeered you won't and*
> *afraid you will,*
> *Just drag to bed and have your*
> *chill,*

> *And pray the Lord to see you*
> *through,*
> *For you've got the Flu, boy,*
> *You've got the Flu. . . .*

> *What is it like, this Spanish Flu?*
> *Ask me, brother, I've been*
> *through.*
> *It is by Misery out of Despair;*
> *It pulls your teeth and curls your*
> *hair;*
> *It thins your blood and brays your*
> *bones,*
> *And fills your craw with moans*
> *and groans,*
> *And sometimes, maybe, you get*
> *well,*
> *Some call it Flu—I call it hell!*[48]

Fighting men dubbed their affliction the "three-day fever" and "knock-me-down fever." Mercifully, first-wave flu caused few deaths. Apparently, the virus had not mutated to the point where victims' immune systems failed to detect it and fight back. Dr. Herbert French, of Britain's Ministry of Health, reported that it caused no complications, which are conditions that worsen an existing infection. Treatment required

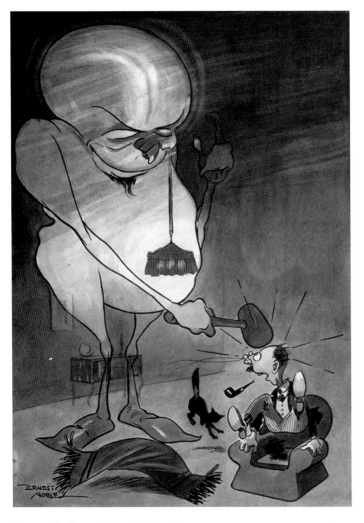

A cartoon by Ernest Noble depicting influenza
as a monster packing a wallop. (1918)

"nothing special," simply "rest in bed for three days and ordinary nursing without drugs."[49]

By early August, new influenza cases had dwindled to nearly zero. A British medical journal reached the logical conclusion, declaring that the disease had "completely disappeared."[50]

But it hadn't.

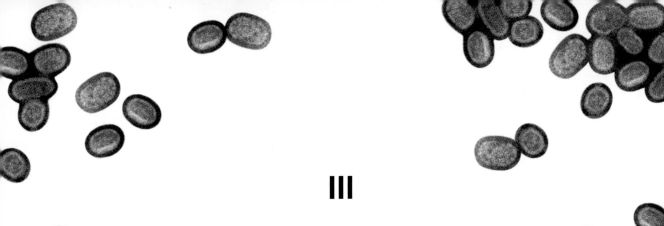

III

PUNY MAN

DROWNING IN THE SECOND WAVE

*It seemed that Nature gathered together all her strength and
demonstrated to man how puny and insignificant he and his fellows are,
with all his murderous machinery, in the destruction of his fellows.*
—Victor C. Vaughan, 1922

BOSTON STRUCK

Somewhere in war-torn France—we will never know exactly where or
when—the Type A H1N1 virus of the first wave shifted, mutating into a mass
murderer of humans. Now better able to evade the immune system and cling
to cell walls, it lodged deep in the lungs, starting its attack there rather than,
as usual, in the throat. Swiftly and savagely, the devil virus sent the second
influenza wave surging across the planet.

In mid-August 1918, seaports on three continents, separated over thousands
of miles by the Atlantic Ocean, felt the fury of the disease. On August 15,
health officials reported a deadly outbreak in the port city of Freetown, Sierra Leone, in West Africa. Exactly a week later, on August 22, flu erupted in
Brest, a French seaport jammed with incoming American troop transports.

The troopship *Mount Vernon* lands Yankee Division troops at Commonwealth Pier in Boston. (1919)

A few days later, it appeared in Boston, Massachusetts. For now, we will focus on Boston, because U.S. army physicians there provided the first detailed accounts of the early stage of the second wave.

U.S. navy ships often sailed home from Brest. Many of them docked at the quarter-mile-long Commonwealth Pier in South Boston. Troops bound for the trenches and returning sailors awaiting other assignments both stayed at a "receiving ship" until their orders came through. This was not a ship at all, but a set of barracks on the pier that housed up to 7,000 men at a time. These barracks were "grossly overcrowded," the navy admitted, cold, drafty, rat-ridden, and foul-smelling. Basic items like soap and toilet paper were scarce; faulty plumbing made toilets overflow. Hot water for a shower was a luxury.[1]

On August 27, two sailors turned up at the Commonwealth Pier's sick bay. One said his illness, whatever it was, felt as if he "had been beaten over the head with a club." The next day, eight other sailors appeared, joined by fifty-eight more the following day. Within a week, the sick bay was swarmed with influenza cases. Unable to handle them all, doctors transferred many to Chelsea Naval Hospital during the first week of September. This move, however, introduced the disease to that hospital—and to patients suffering from other illnesses. Once recovered and discharged, they, in turn, traveled aboard troop trains, often with three men crammed into seats designed to hold two.[2]

Like a spreading ink stain, the virus found its way into civilian communities. Boston reported its first cases on September 3. Bostonians did not take them seriously; the first wave had passed without doing serious harm, and so would this latest outbreak, they hoped. A local newspaper joked about the disease: "Girls of Boston Must Cut Out That Germy Kiss" read the headline. A poster advised:

Avoid the hug,
Avoid the lip,
Escape the bug
That gives the "grippe."[3]

Camp Devens was an army training camp northwest of Boston. Built to house 30,000 recruits but with more than 45,000, it proved that influenza was no laughing matter. Events there showed how lethal the mutated virus had become.

Even before the flu appeared, recruits at Camp Devens were stressed out by the rigorous training program. Starting before sunrise, it went nonstop, with short breaks for hasty meals in the crowded mess halls. After meals, bellowing sergeants put recruits through grueling drills: marching, crawling in mud under machine-gun fire, and firing rifles at "all hours of the day while it was light enough to see a bullseye."[4]

The first flu case at the camp turned up on September 7. The next day, a dozen recruits came to the camp hospital with flu symptoms. Before long, the second wave swamped the place. The hospital overflowed with influenza and pneumonia cases. By the end of October, the hospital counted 17,400 admissions for these diseases. This human deluge stunned Chief Nurse Jane Malloy. "Every inch of available space was used," she recalled, "[so that] three miles of hospital corridors were lined on both sides with cots." Patients' fevers shot up to 104°F, and their bodies ached so that the slightest touch was painful. Deaths skyrocketed, averaging 100 a day. Private Ralph Smith remembered 374 patients dying in a single night. Another soldier exclaimed: "Men were dieing [*sic*] like flys [*sic*], with the flu."[5]

How did they die?

Influenza can kill in two ways. In the first and most common way, deaths are due not to the virus directly but to bacteria that normally live in the noses and throats of healthy people. Such bacteria are harmless if they stay in their proper place. Yet, should the virus attack the cells lining the bronchial (breathing) tubes, the bacteria can move downward, into the lungs. Marvels of natural engineering, our lungs have a combined surface area more than twenty-five times that of our skin. Our lungs also contain 750 million *alveoli,* microscopic air sacs, each as thin and delicate as a soap bubble. When blood passes through the vessels in the lungs, the alveoli transfer oxygen to the red blood cells, which carry it to every cell in our body. Animals and plants need oxygen to stay alive.[6]

Bacterial invaders cause *bacterial pneumonia.* Pneumonia is an infection of the lungs in which the alveoli become inflamed and clogged with pus. As the alveoli fill up, they lose their ability to transfer oxygen to the blood, and the victim grows short of breath. If a person's immune system fails to halt the infection, *cyanosis* develops—a pale blue, purple, or brown tint of the skin. Death, if it comes, does so in about seven to ten days. It comes gently, as the dwindling oxygen supply gradually causes the body to shut down. The victim slips into

a coma, a state of deep unconsciousness (*coma* is from the Greek *koma,* meaning "deep sleep"). Sir William Osler, the English medical genius, thought of pneumonia as merciful. "Pneumonia may well be called the friend of the aged," he wrote a century ago, for it shortens the suffering caused by other diseases, like cancer. In the early 1900s, as today, bacterial pneumonia was the chief killer of the elderly. Even since the discovery of antibiotics in the mid-twentieth century, it claims more Americans of all ages than any other infectious disease—between 40,000 and 70,000 people each year.[7]

The second means of death, *viral pneumonia,* is nobody's friend. In 1918, the mutated Type A H1N1 influenza virus struck in ways physicians had never seen before or thought possible.

At Camp Devens, an army doctor named Roy Grist wrote a fellow physician, describing an alarming new form of cyanosis. Recruits, Grist said, "very rapidly develop the most viscous [thick, sticky, gluey] type of pneumonia that has ever been seen. Two hours after admission they have . . . mahogany spots over the cheek bones, and a few hours later you can begin to see the cyanosis extending from their ears and spreading over the face, until it is hard to distinguish the colored men from the white." This type of cyanosis was a sure death sentence; nobody with it recovered. "It is only a matter of hours," Grist continued, "until death comes and it is simply a struggle for air until they suffocate. It is horrible. One can stand to see one, or two or twenty men die, but to see these poor devils dropping like flies sort of gets on your nerves."[8]

As the disease snuffed out more lives, Grist told his friend, "It takes special trains to carry away the dead. For several days there were no coffins and the bodies piled up something fierce; we used to go down to the morgue and look at the boys laid out in long rows. It beats any sight they ever had in France after a battle. . . . We eat it [influenza], sleep it, and dream it, to say nothing of breathing it 16 hours a day."[9]

Shocked by reports from Massachusetts, the army surgeon general, William Gorgas, sent members of his elite medical team to investigate. "You will," Gorgas ordered, "proceed immediately to Devens. The Spanish influenza has struck the camp." The group included doctors we have already met: Victor Vaughan, William Welch, and Rufus Cole. They arrived on September 23, just sixteen days after the first case checked into the camp hospital.[10]

Deeply learned men, they were experienced in the ways of death. They thought they had seen it all; the study of infectious diseases was woven into the fabric of their adult lives. However, like Roy Grist, what they found at Camp Devens shook them to the core.

The experience burned itself into Victor Vaughan's soul. Memories of that awful place, he wrote years later, were "ghastly ones which I would tear down and destroy were I able to do so, but this is beyond my power. They will be part of my being and will perish only when I die or lose my memory." The doctor said he had haunting visions when he closed his eyes at night: "I see hundreds of young, stalwart men in uniform coming into the wards of the hospital in groups of ten or more. . . . Every bed is full, yet others crowd in. . . . In the morning the dead bodies are stacked about the morgue like cord wood."[11]

Worse scenes awaited the team in the autopsy room. An autopsy is a medical examination of a corpse to discover the cause and manner of death. Autopsies are never pleasant, but those of second-wave flu victims were uniquely horrifying. Just reaching the room was like walking through a nightmare. The team passed bodies laid out on the floor "without any order or system, and . . . had to step amongst them to get into

the room." While one doctor tried to move a corpse aside, "a foamy, blood-stained liquid" ran from its nose and mouth.[12]

Once inside the autopsy room, the doctors found the body of a young soldier lying naked on a wooden table, his head propped up by a wooden block. William Welch, at seventy-one the team's senior member, began the autopsy by opening the chest cavity with a scalpel. When he exposed the lungs, everyone gasped, scarcely able to believe their eyes. Lungs are normally lightweight and billowy, but these were dense purple masses, heavy as slabs of raw liver. Frothy red

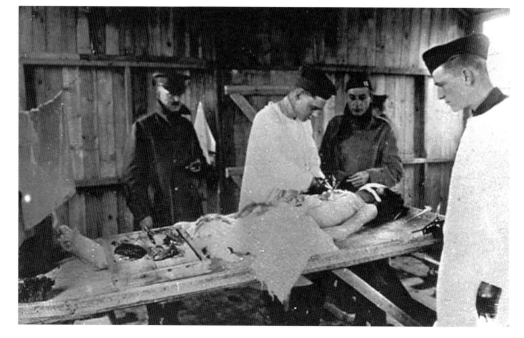

Doctors perform an autopsy at the Kerhuon base hospital in Brest, France. Medical staff there treated more than 3,000 soldiers suffering from influenza and pneumonia, of whom 569 died. Autopsies revealed that influenza victims' lungs appeared strangely blue or purple and were filled with fluid. (Date unknown)

fluid filled the alveoli; the soldier had drowned in his own blood. When placed in buckets of water during autopsies, lungs would ordinarily float; the virus-infected lungs sank to the bottom. Welch was by nature calm and not easily rattled. Now, Rufus Cole said, he turned pale as a bedsheet. "'This must be some new kind of infection or plague,'" Welch said, "and he was quite excited and obviously very nervous. . . . It was not surprising that the rest of us were disturbed, and it shocked me to find that the situation . . . was too much even for Dr. Welch."[13]

But Welch was wrong: this was not a new kind of infection, but an old one turned vicious by a mutated virus, a thing nobody knew existed. That an expert like Welch should have suggested plague as a cause further highlights the huge gap in the medical profession's knowledge. Though physicians saw influenza's ravages in the autopsy room, they could not explain why or how these came about.

Scientists today believe the virus did its worst damage by triggering a *cytokine storm,* which turned victims' own immune systems against them.

Cytokines, we recall, are chemical messengers that alert the immune system and send aid to the site of an infection. However, there can be too much of a good thing. Sometimes cytokines send huge amounts of immune cells flooding into the lungs. Then, for reasons still unclear, the cytokines overreact, "ordering" uncontrolled amounts of these cells to fight the infection. As the overreaction intensifies, immune cells spread throughout the body, attacking every organ and causing sudden, violent death.

That is what happened in 1918. Influenza victims developed gruesome symptoms. We have reports of blood vessels leaking, causing blood to pour from noses, mouths, ears, and eye sockets. Coughing became pure agony. American author John Dos Passos, who barely survived, remembered, "I coughed in a manner to turn my throat inside out and then outside in again." In some cases, violent coughing ruptured stomach muscles, tore apart the muscles of the rib cage, and broke ribs. Lungs collapsed, trapping air bubbles beneath the skin. "As we rolled the dead in winding sheets," a nurse recalled, "their bodies crackled—an awful crackling noise which sounded like Rice Crispies [*sic*] when you pour milk over them." Some doctors and nurses died the same way.[14]

Another strange aspect of the mutated virus was the ages of its victims. Graphs of age-related flu deaths usually follow the trend of a U-shaped curve, as shown by the dotted line on the graph below, with peaks for babies and toddlers under the age of five and for old people over the age of sixty-five. The reason is probably that the immune systems of the very young are not fully developed, and advancing age weakens the immune systems of the elderly. Normally, when young adults catch influenza, they recover. This pattern changed during the second wave. It created a spike in the middle, the crude W-shaped curve shown by the solid line, represent-

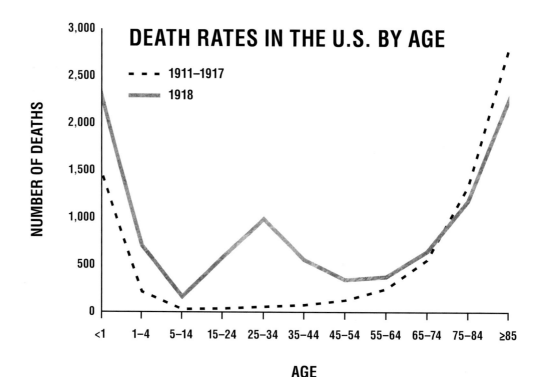

ing those between ages eighteen and thirty-five. In other words, people in the prime of life were now at grave risk. Their death rates were several times higher than usual, most likely because their immune systems, operating at peak strength, triggered cytokine storms.[15]

PANDEMIC

Influenza raged at Camp Devens until late October. But it did not stay there. As during the first wave, the constant movement of recruits carried the virus to every military base and training camp in the country. Replacements from Camp Devens, for example, brought it to Camp Upton on Long Island, New York, a jumping-off point for troopships bound for Europe. As flu blazed through the camp, Naomi Barnett of Brockton, Massachusetts, rushed to care for her fiancé, Jacob Julian, when she learned of his condition. They planned to be married before he shipped out for France, but the bride-to-be died of flu-related pneumonia two days after her arrival. The love of her life died a half hour later. "Relatives," their hometown newspaper reported, "are planning a double funeral in Brockton." Overwhelmed and feeling powerless against the disease, Colonel Charles B. Hagadorn, the camp commander, put a bullet into his brain.[16]

Because of the raging pandemic, medical personnel worked extended shifts. At the Great Lakes Naval Training Station north of Chicago, Josie Mabel Brown put in sixteen-hour days as a nurse, she told an interviewer in 1986, the year she turned 100. "There were so many patients we didn't have time to treat them," Brown said. "We didn't take temperatures; we didn't even have time to take blood pressure. We would give them a little hot whiskey toddy; that's about all we had time to do. They would have terrific nosebleeds . . . [and] sometimes blood would just shoot across the room. You had to get out of the way or someone's nose would bleed all over you." With its hospitals overwhelmed, the army put flu patients in jam-packed gymnasiums. Hundreds of men lay in cots, just inches apart, coughing and sneezing, separated only by bedsheets draped across ropes.[17]

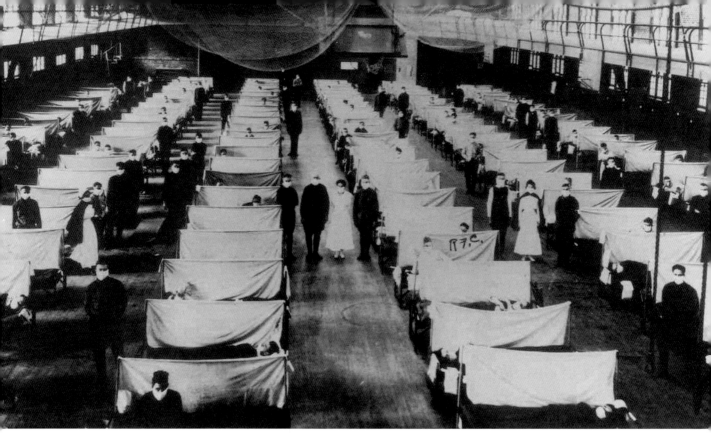

As influenza spread in 1919, any available space became an impromptu medical ward.

Upon seeing a patient with a purple face, Brown knew he bore the mark of death. Though alive when he arrived, he was a goner; he had only hours left, or a day at most. When death came, nurses wrapped the body in a winding sheet, Brown said, "and left nothing but the big toe on his left foot out with a shipping tag on it to tell the man's rank, his nearest of kin, and hometown." Death struck so quickly that "the morgues were packed almost to the ceiling with bodies stacked one on top of another." She said she felt sorry for "the poor fellow at the bottom of the heap."[18]

"The Flu," a poem by Private Josh Lee, captures the epidemic's impact on an ordinary recruit:

> It stalked into camp when the day
>   was damp
> And chilly and cold.
> It crept by the guards
> And murdered my pards
> With a hand that was clammy
>   and bony and bold;

And its breath was icy and
  mouldy and dank,
And it killed so speedy
And gloatingly greedy
That it took away men from each
  company rank.[19]

Nothing could check the viral rampage. In the United States, H1N1 put no fewer than 675,000 civilians into graveyards. This is a staggering number, more than the nation's total military deaths in World War I, World War II, the Korean War, and the Vietnam War combined. Our neighbor to the north, Canada, a vast but thinly populated country of 8.1 million, lost about 50,000 people. In Montreal in November, an eyewitness reported, "funerals became so numerous that cemetery officials could not dispose of the corpses fast enough." That same month, the Reverend Henry Gordon made his rounds in Labrador, a rural province with remote logging camps and fishing villages. Gordon found villages where "whole households lay inanimate on their kitchen floors, unable to feed even themselves or look after the fire."[20]

Sailors aboard cargo ships brought the infection to Latin America. Mexico saw influenza race through its towns and cities, all but crippling Mexico City, the capital. The virus struck peasant farmers, the poorest of the poor, and the masters of haciendas—sprawling ranches and estates with grand houses dating from Spanish colonial days. In the state of Chiapas, in the southeast on the border with Guatemala, 10 percent of the population died. By the time the second wave passed, the flu had claimed more than 300,000 Mexican lives.[21]

Next the virus found its way into British Guiana (now Guyana), a British colony on the northeast coast of South America. "The epidemic has been the most severe visitation within the memory of any colonist," a public health officer reported. "The almost universal prevalence and high mortality rate have caused untold suffering." The virus killed 12,000 out of a population of 310,000. Farther south, in Brazil, 350,000 died, including Francisco de Paula Rodrigues Alves, the nation's president-elect.[22]

Central America and the islands

of the Caribbean fared no better. Ships carried the infection to British Honduras (now Belize), a small country in Central America, bordered by Mexico on the north and the Caribbean Sea on the east. "The catastrophe," a British newspaper observed, "came and went, a hurricane across the green fields of life." A banana-boat crew brought the virus to the island of Jamaica; it killed 10,000 out of a population of 850,000. In all, influenza claimed the lives of around 100,000 people in the Caribbean region.[23]

Meanwhile, the mutated virus fastened its hold on Europe. No fewer than 250,000 people died in Great Britain. In the autumn of 1918, bacterial pneumonia and influenza carried away 18,000 Londoners. Their city had so many cases that the London Zoo in Regents Park enclosed its monkeys in glass cages to protect them from infected visitors. A young woman named Caroline Playne, an avid diary keeper, wrote: "In trains and trams, the depression shown on travelers' faces was very noticeable and talk was all about specially sad cases of death from influenza. A sense of dread is very general."

And no wonder, because such an authority as Sir Bertrand Dawson, the king's personal physician, admitted defeat. "I fail to see any explanation [for the disease]," the learned doctor said after examining patients.[24]

The disease easily crossed the Irish Sea from Great Britain to the Emerald Isle. Ireland's official death toll was 23,288, but researchers believe the actual number was much higher. Molly Deery, from County Donegal, on the northwest coast, recalled the flu experience years later. The disease "hit hard and the people were very fearful and frightened of it. You see the people had no idea what caused it. . . . It was terrible, terrible . . . and people were told to keep to one side of the road if someone in a house had it." People in Dublin, the capital, believed the disease originated in the trenches of the Western Front. A press report said that a Dublin doctor, home on leave, "found within the past week several cases of 'influenza' in which the 'symptoms' are very similar to those observed in soldiers 'gassed' in the trenches." He was right in one sense: victims of both gas poisoning and influenza often turned blue or purple.[25]

In continental Europe, influenza killed more than 240,000 French men and women; in Paris alone, 1,200 people died each week. Germany lost more than twice that number: 562,000. Hardly any German family escaped an encounter with the devil virus. "From our housekeeper," a wealthy woman wrote, "I hear that the whole village is stricken with it, and the wretched people are lying on the floors of their cottages in woeful heaps, shivering with fever and with no [medicine] or any one to attend them." Italy, which fought on the Allied side, lost slightly fewer than Germany: 544,000 during the pandemic. Neutral Spain counted over 260,000 deaths from flu and bacterial pneumonia.[26]

AFRICAN HOLOCAUST

The term *holocaust* means "total destruction by fire." Nowadays, the *Holocaust* (with a capital *H*) refers to German dictator Adolf Hitler's attempt to exterminate Europe's Jews and other "racially inferior" groups as part of his plan for world conquest during the Second World War. It is not too much to say that, for Africa, the influenza pandemic was a natural holocaust because it took so many lives, especially of black people ruled by foreigners.

In 1918, the African continent had only one independent country: Ethiopia. During the half century before the First World War, Europeans carried out a wild "Scramble for Africa," seizing all the lands south of the Sahara. Great Britain, France, Belgium, Italy, and Germany ruled colonies with millions of native people and untold natural resources. To make this vast area governable and profitable, the imperial powers linked their holdings with seaports and railroads. However, these facilities, so vital to the continent's economic development, had an unforeseen effect. As one historian observed, it was as if "the colonial transportation network had been planned in preparation for the pandemic." Africa, where the human race originated over a million years ago, had never seen anything like this monster.[27]

The trouble began in August 1918 in West Africa. The *Mantua,* a British warship, had docked at Freetown, Sierra Leone, to take on a supply of coal. But the *Mantua* was not a happy ship; a third of the crew, 124 sailors,

HMS *Mantua.*
(1914)

lay in their hammocks, coughing and burning with fever. Rather than place the *Mantua* under strict quarantine, port authorities, afraid of hampering naval operations, ordered black dockworkers to load the coal. They fell ill almost immediately, carrying the devil virus to Freetown's population. "The disease," the British governor reported, "spread with devastating rapidity, disorganizing everything. Everybody was attacked almost at once."[28]

From Freetown, H1N1 traveled along the coast and inland by way of ships, trains, and riverboats. Infected sailors aboard other British warships also brought it to Gambia, north of Sierra Leone. A traveler reported from the Gambian interior: "I found whole villages of 300 to 400 families completely wiped out, the houses having fallen in on the unburied dead, and the jungle having crept in within two months, obliterating whole settlements." Survivors had become pitiful scarecrows, shadows of their former selves. A British medical officer wrote, "Individuals who prior to an attack were strong, burly, healthy persons, in a few days became emaciated wrecks of humanity, barely able to crawl, and unable to undertake the slightest amount of exertion."[29]

To the east of Sierra Leone, Nigeria lay in the path of the infection. Nigerians called it *lululuka* (killing by a sudden stroke) and *ajukale-arun* (a disease that spreads everywhere). To ward it off, Muslims in Lagos, the capital, drank water in which pages from the Quran, Islam's holy book, had been dipped. Nigeria had the largest population in black Africa. Of its 18.6 million people, the best estimate is that 455,000 died, the vast majority of them black.[30]

British ships brought the virus to South Africa in October. Located at the southern tip of the continent, it was a self-governing country within the British Empire. The richest and most highly developed area south of the Sahara, it held invaluable mineral resources: diamonds, gold, platinum, copper, coal, iron ore—all mined by black workers directed by white bosses.

South Africans, whatever their color, remember October 1918 as "Black October." It was a dark time, the darkest ever recorded there. Influenza first struck Cape Town, the country's largest city and main seaport. Native people called it *kaapito hanga* (it came fast as a bullet). Deaths rocketed to 500 a day, and within two weeks Cape Town "was like a city of the dead." Its main streets, usually bustling and crowded, were all but deserted at midday. People stayed home, worrying, "and nothing [was] talked of or thought about other than influenza."[31]

But this was just the beginning.

Before long, the virus invaded the South African countryside. In rural areas, cows lowed in pain as their udders swelled with milk. "A solemn hush prevailed," a white farmer scrawled in his diary. "No one to be seen, no one to be heard; no life on the farms, no work in the lands. Lord influenza and his followers have . . . the countryside in their grip." His Lordship took the lives of at least 300,000 of South Africa's 6.7 million people. Deaths from starvation soared, too, because farmers were too sick to harvest or plant their crops. Most starvation victims, however, were black people. White settlers could afford to buy expensive food imported from Europe.[32]

In early November, the virus reached East Africa by railroad, by sea, and in the bodies of migrant workers returning home. Advancing northward, it terrorized Tanganyika (today's Tanzania), a German colony conquered by British forces. Though the number of dead is unclear, travelers reported the disease "strewing the road with dead and dying." Things were no better in neighboring Kenya, where 150,000 perished. Nairobi, the capital of Kenya and the British colony's largest white settlement, was then little more than a village set in the wilds. It was not unusual to see a herd of zebra running down its main street in broad daylight. One never knew what to expect at night. Occasionally, a lion wandered in from the plains, hungry for household pets and unwary townspeople. Yet flu proved deadlier than any big cat. Ditto for Kenya's northern neighbor, Ethiopia. The emperor, known as the "Lion of Judah," sat on his jeweled throne, helpless. Years afterward, residents recalled that the capital, Addis Ababa, "looked like a dead city." Influenza made even the government shut down, and in 1918 and 1919, Ethiopia had more deaths than births.[33]

White Christians often explained the disaster in a time-honored way: it was God's punishment of humanity for its sins. To the seven deadly sins—anger, greed, lust, envy, pride, laziness, gluttony—they added an eighth sin: "worshipping science." A South African preacher declared from the pulpit: "Nowadays people speak of germs and filthy streets and slums [as causes of disease]. But God

wants us to have no other Gods than Him." Another preacher blamed science for both the war and the pandemic. "Isn't it as if the Almighty is toying with the murder resulting from sinful science?" he asked. "Humans may kill thousands, but God can kill in tens of thousands." Thus, the only cure for the pandemic was to "get right" with the Lord.[34]

Black people held two different views of the pandemic. In 1918, traditional African religion was still a powerful force. It taught that illness did not just happen but struck because someone magically "sent" it to do harm. Despite Christian missionaries attempting to convert the locals, witch finders—people claiming to have supernatural powers—still "smelled out" witches and wizards, literally sniffed them to detect the unique "odor" of evil. "Many cases of homicide or serious assault," a South African official reported, "resulting from 'smelling out' have come to my notice recently, especially after the outbreak of influenza in the native territories."[35]

However, other native Africans blamed the disaster on the war. When

British troops seized Germany's colonies, black soldiers fought beside them, and black teamsters hauled military supplies. When influenza struck, it was so beyond blacks' experience that they decided the war must be to blame. It was dubbed the "White Man's Flu" and "war air" because many thought smoke from the big guns had fouled the air in a way that made it poisonous. Some went further, claiming a more sinister cause. "This disease," they insisted, "was a device of the Europeans to finish off the Native races of South Africa." Similarly, some whites, though ignorant of influenza's true cause, blamed it on blacks' "racial inferiority" and disregard of basic hygiene. To safeguard the health of whites, they demanded the separation of the races. Though apartheid, the South African government's policy of rigid racial segregation, did not officially begin until 1948, its roots went back thirty years, to the influenza pandemic.[36]

THE KILLER CIRCLES THE GLOBE

Influenza spread eastward from Africa, across the Indian Ocean, to India, in South Asia. Known as the "Jewel in the Crown," British-ruled India was the empire's largest and most valuable holding in 1918. English is still the country's second language, and the railroads built by the colonial rulers still flourish.

H1N1 first came ashore at Bombay (today's Mumbai), a sprawling seaport on the country's west coast. From there, it spread north, south, and east, carried by infected train and riverboat passengers. In its wake, it left human devastation on a scale never before seen in India, a land often racked by crop failures and famines. Influenza's effects reminded followers of Hinduism, India's chief religion, of a saying by the god Vishnu. In a Hindu sacred text, Vishnu proclaims, "I am death, the mighty destroyer of the world, out to destroy." For devout Hindus, it seemed as if only a divine force could unleash such horrors.[37]

The pandemic rolled across India, unstoppable by human ingenuity or prayers. In Bombay, the largest city, 700 people died in a single day. On India's east coast, a muddy river flowing through the port city of Calcutta

SPREAD OF THE INFLUENZA PANDEMIC OF 1918

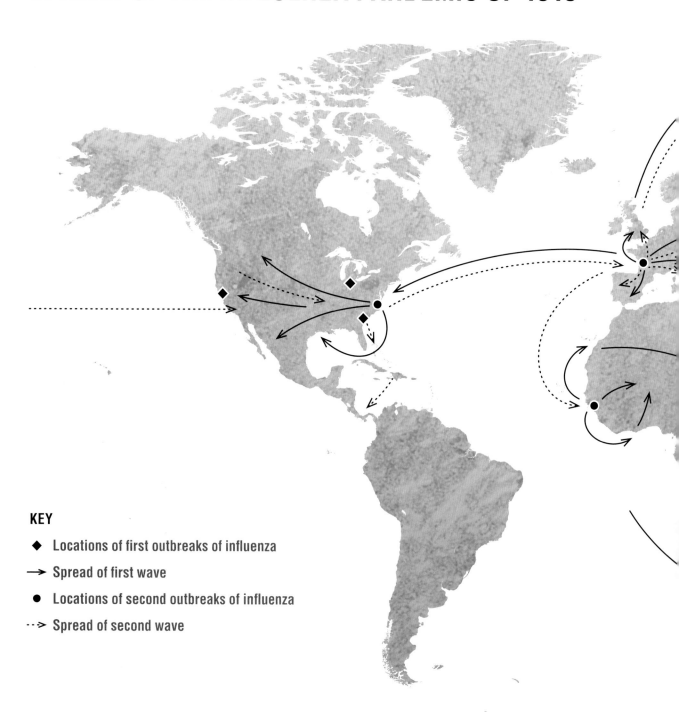

KEY

◆ Locations of first outbreaks of influenza

→ Spread of first wave

● Locations of second outbreaks of influenza

--→ Spread of second wave

(today's Kolkata) into the Bay of Bengal was "choked with bodies."[38]

With many of India's physicians, native-born and white, serving overseas with the British army, people lacked basic medical care. The Associated Press reported that across the country "hospitals were so choked it was impossible quickly to remove the dead and make room for the dying. Streets and lanes of the cities were littered with dead and dying people. . . . The depleted medical service, itself severely stricken by the epidemic, was incapable of dealing with more than a minute fraction of the sick requiring attention." No country suffered worse than India. An astounding 6.1 percent, or 18.6 million, of its 305.6 million people died of influenza. In other words, India lost twice as many civilians as all soldiers killed during the World War.[39]

H1N1 continued its lethal journey. Ships brought it across the South China Sea to the bustling seaport of Hong Kong, China. Though China had a larger population than India, 472 million in 1918, influenza claimed fewer victims, an estimated 9.5 million, for reasons that are still unclear.

Influenza also reached Japan, an Allied power, by way of China or Allied ships, or both; 388,000 Japanese died. "The misery is appalling," official reports said. Vessels also brought the mutated virus to the Philippines (93,686 died). The Dutch East Indies (today's Indonesia) lost 1.5 million of its 30 million inhabitants.[40]

Australia and New Zealand were next in line. Immense areas, sparsely populated, these island nations counted around 23,100 deaths. Like Cape Town, Wellington, New Zealand's capital, seemed deserted. Businessman Alfred Hollows recalled: "I stood in the middle of Wellington City at 2 p.m. on a weekday afternoon, and there was not a soul to be seen—no trams running, no shops open, and the only traffic was a van with a white sheet tied to its side, and a big red cross painted on it, serving as an ambulance or hearse. It was really a City of the Dead."[41]

Other islands fared far worse. Fiji, today's Republic of the Fiji Islands, a country in the South Pacific Ocean east of Australia, consists of more than 300 widely scattered islands. In the sixteen days following November 25, 1918, influenza swept away

9,000 out of a total of 164,000 Fijians. An Australian visitor to a sugar plantation on one island reported: "For a full week I was the only person moving about in this particular district. Everything was still and quiet. Cattle were unattended and helped themselves to growing crops of rice and sugar-cane. Bananas ripened on the trees and afterward turned to vinegar on the ground.... [Yet] there was any amount of noise all night long—the hacking cough of the unfortunates who had developed pneumonia as a complication." From Suva, Fiji's capital, a visitor wrote, "Day and night trucks rumbled through the streets, filled with bodies for constantly burning pyres."[42]

Similar accounts came from every part of the globe. Mysterious and merciless, untreatable and unstoppable, the pandemic had the upper hand. Thoughtful people, continents and oceans apart, asked the same questions and arrived at the same answers as Europeans had during the Black Death. In West Africa's Gold Coast, for instance, villagers wondered "if this [was] the end of the world," and a black South African thought the pandemic "threaten[ed] the existence of the entire [human] race."[43]

Here we will give the last word to Victor Vaughan. One night, the noted physician sat alone in his office, brooding. Vaughan knew as much about infectious diseases as anyone on the planet in 1918. He also knew how to count and how to project his findings into the future. He scribbled this on a piece of paper: "If the epidemic continues its mathematical rate of acceleration, civilization could easily disappear... from the face of the earth within a matter of a few more weeks."[44]

IV

A FEAR AND PANIC

INFLUENZA AND AMERICAN SOCIETY

A fear and panic of the influenza, akin to the terror of the Middle Ages regarding the Black Plague, [has] been prevalent in many parts of the country.
—American Red Cross report, 1918

SCIENTIFIC MEDICINE'S FAILURE

American physicians, like their European colleagues, entered the twentieth century justly proud of the triumphs of scientific medicine. In the decades before World War I, they had discovered the causes of many diseases, conquered pain, and promoted public health. And now this! Never in modern times had there been such a crisis in which physicians felt so helpless, so unprepared to deal with a disease of such a horrific nature.

Victor Vaughan was downcast. Witnessing the pandemic was, he recalled in his autobiography, "the saddest part of my life." If medicine's failure taught him anything, he confessed, it was humility. "I decided," he wrote, "never again to prate about the great achievements of medical science and to humbly admit our dense ignorance in [this] case." Vaughan's friend William Welch agreed.

The pandemic, said the famous pathologist, would forever remain the "great shadow cast upon the medical profession." Other physicians, overcome by despair, wondered why they had devoted their lives to medicine. "Why did I become a doctor?" one muttered. "I can do nothing to help, and soon there won't be any more people."[1]

As we have seen, neither physicians nor the public they served knew the cause of influenza. A bit of dark humor expressed their puzzlement. In November 1918, as the war's end drew near, the *Illinois Health News* printed this anonymous poem:

?Flu?
If we but knew
The cause of flu
And whence it comes and what
  to do,
I think that you
And we folks , too,
Would hardly get in such a stew.
Do you?

Flu came from *something*—that was common sense, a logical matter of cause and effect. But without hard scientific facts about viruses, one explanation seemed as credible as the next. It was simply a case of believing whatever you wished, whatever satisfied you or gave you peace of mind.[2]

POPULAR EXPLANATIONS

In seeking to explain the disease, many Americans saw it in terms of their long-held prejudices. Since colonial times, America has attracted immigrants in search of freedom and opportunity. In the beginning, most immigrants came from western and northern Europe: Great Britain, Germany, Scandinavia. In the 1880s, however, a flood of immigrants started arriving from eastern and southern Europe, chiefly Russia and Italy. These newcomers—Jews and Roman Catholics in a Protestant-majority country—spoke languages and had customs different from those of self-styled "real Americans." Worse, this "foreign element" gained a reputation as disease carriers.

Many Jews suffered from tuberculosis, dubbed the "Jewish disease." Tuberculosis raged among Jews who lived in crowded urban tenements and worked long hours for low pay in unhealthy factories called sweatshops. Moreover, critics charged, "the Jewish body was inherently inferior to the Christian body."[3]

Most Italians had emigrated from southern Italy, a region racked by poverty, illiteracy, and superstition. Southern Italians believed in the *malocchio* (evil eye), the ability to harm others simply by looking at them with envy. Italians also had strong family bonds, gathering around the beds of the sick to comfort them and kissing the dead to express grief and respect. Given their peculiar illnesses and customs, Jews and Italians were denounced as "society's dregs" and thus were judged to be especially prone to contagious diseases. By this twisted logic, they were breeding grounds for influenza.[4]

Other Americans blamed the pandemic on Germany, an idea that fit neatly with the demands of waging the war. The conflict's outcome was not simply a matter of soldiers winning battles. It also depended on civilians on the home front believing in the Allied cause and being willing to give their labor, their wealth, and their menfolk for the glory of "God and country."

To keep Americans believing and giving, in 1917 President Wilson created the Committee on Public Information (CPI), the nation's first propaganda agency. Using newspapers, films, posters, songs, and trained speakers, CPI experts stressed two themes: (1) The Allies were just, humane, and moral. (2) The Germans were the exact opposite—despicable, cruel, and corrupt. A poster from that time, colorful and shocking, says it all. Used to encourage army enlistments, it shows Germany as a howling, drooling, club-waving gorilla grasping a half-naked woman covering her eyes in terror. Its orange letters say: "Destroy This Mad Brute—Enlist." To sell Liberty Bonds to pay for the war, movie stars Charlie Chaplin and Douglas Fairbanks harangued crowds and posed for advertisements. A grim poster shows German bombers reducing the Statue of Liberty to ruins. Its caption reads: "That Liberty Shall Not Perish from the Earth—Buy Liberty Bonds." Never mind that no airplane could fly across the Atlantic Ocean in 1918.

For propagandists, whatever promoted the Allied cause was true, whether factual or not. What counted was the noble end—victory—not the

LEFT: A poster depicting Germany as a monstrous beast. (1917)

RIGHT: Charlie Chaplin stumps for Liberty Bonds in *The Bond,* a film he made at his own expense to help the war effort. (1918)

sordid means of achieving it. "Truth and falsehood are arbitrary terms," declared a CPI official. "There is nothing in experience to tell us that one is always preferable to the other. . . . There are lifeless truths and vital lies. . . . The force of an idea lies in its inspirational value. It matters very little if it is true or false."[5]

God, too, became part of the propaganda effort. Depending on where you heard it, the Almighty was British, French, Belgian, Russian, Austrian, or German. Not to be outdone, American clergymen of all denomi-nations became superpatriots. A poet-priest put it like this:

> *Fight for the colors of Christ the*
> *King,*
> *Fight as He fought for you;*
> *Fight for the Right with all your*
> *might,*
> *Fight for the Red, White, and*
> *Blue.*[6]

The Reverend Billy Sunday, a baseball player turned popular preacher, appealed to countless American Christians. Love of the United States and love of the Lord,

BILLY SUNDAY
FIGHTING the DEVIL

A *Detroit News Tribune* spread of the Reverend Billy Sunday "fighting the devil." (1916)

Sunday said, were really the same. "I am glad that loyalty to my country and to Jesus Christ are synonymous," he told thousands, "Germany against America, hell against heaven." America, he added, had a divine mission to crush the "devil hordes," those "dirty Germans," those "hungry hyenas," those beasts "out of the pits of hell." Just as Germany had used poison gas first, Sunday insisted, it had unleashed influenza, too. The pandemic "started over there in Spain," the preacher thundered from the pulpit, "where they [Germans] scattered germs around. . . . There's nothing short of hell they haven't stooped to since the war began." Forget that influenza ravaged Germany

as badly as it attacked any other European country. For Billy Sunday and his kind, the will to believe overcame awkward facts.[7]

The idea of Germany's guilt for the pandemic gained wide acceptance. Even respected newspapers like the *New York Times* blamed Germany. "Let the curse be called the German plague," the *Times* declared with all the confidence of ignorance. Others, equally confident, insisted that Bayer aspirin had become a weapon. The popular drug was manufactured in the United States under a German license, and critics said the formula had been secretly laced with "germs."[8]

The threat of influenza terrorism kept the country on edge. A German ship supposedly sneaked into Boston Harbor one night and released the germs that infected the city. An elderly woman said she saw it release a gray cloud that drifted over the waterfront.[9]

With German submarines prowling the Atlantic coast, some military officers linked the pandemic to the undersea raiders. Colonel Philip S. Doane of the Emergency Fleet Corporation, which oversaw American shipyards, told the newspapers: "It is quite possible that the epidemic was started by [agents] sent ashore by submarine commanders.... It would be quite easy for one of these agents to turn loose those Spanish influenza germs in a theater or some other place where large numbers of persons are assembled.... The Germans have started epidemics in Europe, and there is no reason why they should be particularly gentle with America." Newspapers quickly spread Doane's theory across the country.[10]

Colonel Doane was wrong. There was (and is) no proof that German agents deliberately infected anybody in Europe with bacteria, let alone with a virus. Yet that did not put a stop to the rumors. One particularly nasty rumor claimed that "almost every U.S. Army Camp" had seen executions of traitors—doctors and nurses who had injected recruits with influenza germs. Ordinary folks took to calling Germany "*Germ*-any." A newspaper article titled "The Germs Are Coming" warned of an enemy invasion by influenza, not troops. All of which confirms the proverb "The first casualty of war is truth."[11]

The World War I U-boat *UB 14*. One theory held that German U-boats released the influenza virus on American shores. (1918)

"PREVENTION," "TREATMENT," AND "CURE"

Everyone believed, but no one could yet prove, that influenza, whatever caused it, passed from person to person. As had happened during the plague years of the Middle Ages, authorities in 1918 tried to curb influenza by limiting human contact. The U.S. surgeon general, Rupert Blue, set the tone. On October 4, 1918, he recommended closing "all public gathering places" where the disease might spread. Note: *recommended,* not *ordered.* Blue's lack of action typified poor leadership in high places; indeed, no single official took charge of the anti-flu effort. Throughout the pandemic, the

Surgical masks supposedly provided protection against the killer flu for American baseball players. (1918)

Influenza forced many theaters, shops, restaurants, and other gathering spots to close. (1918)

nation lacked a uniform policy about gathering places, and there was no central authority with the power to make and enforce rules that everyone had to obey. Each community acted on its own, doing as its elected officials thought best.[12]

New York, the nation's largest city, offers a perfect example of this problem. City officials sent out mixed messages. Public libraries, the New York Stock Exchange, and private clubs had to close their doors. Telephone booths were padlocked, and drinking fountains were cleansed every few hours with blowtorches. But officials allowed subways, streetcars, churches, department stores, and factories to stay open, along with saloons, which workers insisted they needed to relax in after a hard day on the job. Workmen marched with NO BEER, NO WORK buttons on their overalls. In Little Italy, a large immigrant neighborhood, you could hardly find a store without a NO WINE, NO WEDDING sign in its window. In Italian-immigrant culture, gathering to drink wine played an important role on joyful occasions like weddings and christenings.[13]

Across the nation, places of amusement were hard-hit. Concert halls, dance halls, pool halls, circuses, skating rinks, public playgrounds, swimming pools, and county fairs had to shut down. New York City's Broadway, the "Great White Way" lined with theaters, went dark. Because of movie-house closings, the fledgling motion picture industry came to a standstill. Gloom settled over Hollywood. Stars like Mary Pickford, "America's Sweetheart," found themselves without paychecks, as did thousands of lesser folks: writers, musicians, camera crews, theater employees. As reported in *Moving Picture World,* the industry newspaper, before closing his theater, an owner with a sense of humor flashed a message on the screen:

Old Mother Hubbard went to the
    cupboard
To get her dog a stew.
When she got there she tore her
    hair,
For the stew had the Spanish Flu.

Little Miss Muffett sat on a tuffet,
The tuffet was covered with dew.
Along came a spider and sat down
    beside her

And they both caught the Spanish Flu.

Hark! Hark! The dogs do bark
The Flu is coming to town.
"We'll close the show till it goes,"
Said the hell-th board.[14]

Officials in some communities decided to bar outsiders entirely. The town of Gunnison, Colorado, for instance, isolated itself "against the world," residents boasted. Sheriff's deputies set up roadblocks, preventing motorists from entering town. When trains stopped to unload freight, conductors reminded passengers that they faced arrest, a stiff fine, and five days in quarantine if they stepped onto the platform to stretch their legs. Another Colorado town, Ouray, in the San Juan Mountains, went further. Ouray's sheriff hired guards to enforce a "shotgun" quarantine against outsiders. No matter: influenza got in anyway, infecting 150 townspeople. St. Louis, Missouri, barred soldiers and sailors on leave from entering the city.[15]

Newspapers printed articles about families barricading themselves in their homes, a strategy tried in the

THE WAY THE GERMANS DID IT AT CHATEAU-THIERRY

During the recent war approximately 1000 men from North Carolina were killed in battle.

THE WAY NORTH CAROLINIANS DO IT AT HOME

During the epidemic last fall and winter 13,644 North Carolinians laid down their lives to a "spit-borne" disease—influenza !

A pair of cartoons from the *Health Bulletin* warning North Carolinians about the spread of influenza. (1919)

where the germs were coming from. We only knew the germs were carried by the air and had gotten into our house. We plugged up the keyholes with cotton so air couldn't get in, sealed the doors and the cracks around the doors because we thought the outside air was contaminated. One particular family, I remember, closed up every possible avenue of letting fresh air into the house.... They plugged up keyholes on the door, sealed windows, and stayed inside, breathing their own air.[16]

plague years of the Middle Ages. The reason, one explained, was that "a little fresh air could be fatal." Years later, Lee Reay of Meadow, Utah, described what it was like to hole up during the influenza panic:

No one had ever seen the germs of the disease. No one knew

Families might seal their homes too well; some died of suffocation, especially if they used oxygen-gulping kerosene lamps. Yet the opposite was true in New York City. At Roosevelt Hospital, children suffering from influenza got the "roof treatment." Nurses put the feverish youngsters to bed on the hospital's roof with hot-water bottles, surrounded by screens to shelter them from the icy winds blowing off the Hudson River. Most of the children recovered.[17]

Before the pandemic, Americans regarded unprotected coughing and sneezing as bad manners. Now they saw these, along with spitting, as crimes. Everywhere signs condemned "open-faced sneezers." Buses and streetcars were plastered with a three-word slogan: SPIT SPREADS DEATH. Billboards along New York streets warned: "It Is Unlawful to Cough and Sneeze"; violators faced a $500 fine (a huge sum in 1918) and a year in jail. Chicago officials went all out, ordering the police to "arrest thousands, if necessary, to stop the sneezing in public!" The front doors of churches bore announcements such as this:

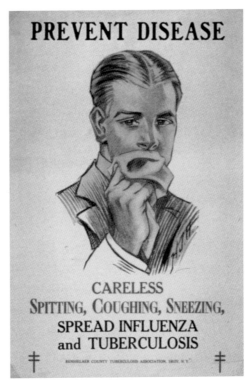

A public health poster cautioning against careless ways of spreading the flu. (1925)

NOTICE
Any person having a cough or cold
is not permitted
to enter this Church.

Anti-sneezing rules proved a blessing to hooky players: inhaling a pinch of pepper became a get-out-of-school-for-the-day pass.[18]

Shielding one's face with a handkerchief when coughing or sneezing became a patriotic duty. Cartoons aimed at children taught the importance of the "snot rag." My favorite shows a boy with a regular-size handkerchief asking his friend with a towel-size one: "Did ya get that fer yer birthday? Gee! That's some handkerchief." His proud friend replies: "Yeh, me mother made it fer me. It's good for a hundred sneezes." Posters of a dapper fellow covering his mouth with a handkerchief read: "Prevent Disease—Careless Spitting, Coughing, Sneezing, Spread Influenza and Tuberculosis." Health officials urged that handkerchiefs "should be placed in boiling water as soon as possible after use."[19]

Face masks became the rage. Made of gauze, a type of loosely woven lightweight cotton fabric, surgical masks were standard in hospital operating rooms by 1918; doctors and nurses wore them to filter out dust and bacteria. However, the pandemic made masks, praised as "little gauze germ catchers," essential for everyone. The American Red Cross and private companies turned them out by the millions. Sold for a dime, masks came in three styles. The Agincourt had a pointed snout, like the helmets worn by French knights at the time of the Black Death. The Ravioli was a square slab, popular with police officers. The Yashmak, modeled on harem-style women's veils, was long, reaching below the chin.[20]

People wore face masks everywhere: postal workers making deliveries, secretaries sitting at their desks, police officers on patrol, teachers in classrooms, and courting couples kissing. At baseball games, where allowed, players wore masks. Some imaginative people decorated theirs with a skull and crossbones, pirate-style, or a pink propeller, clown-style. Cigarette addicts had masks with a little round hole cut in front of their mouths to allow for inhaling the smoke and blowing it out. Criminals wore masks during holdups; since masks were so common, few paid attention to masked men walking the streets in broad daylight. Masks, however, did not raise people's spirits. In Colorado Springs, for example, the local newspaper deplored "a city of masked faces, a city as grotesque as a masked carnival."[21]

San Francisco became mask-crazed. Mayor James Rolph announced, "Who leaves his mask behind, dies." Villains called "mask slackers" were hauled into court and fined for the offense. A jingle blessed by the city fathers went:

Obey the laws
And wear the gauze
Protect your jaws
From septic paws.

Mask slacking was a serious offense, which explains why the police looked the other way when a health department inspector shot a blacksmith for refusing to "wear the gauze."[22]

In San Francisco, as throughout the nation, medical authorities, government officials, and the media supported the wearing of masks as a nearly foolproof way of avoiding the dread disease. Newspaper advertisements blared: "Wear a Mask and Save Your Life!" A gauze mask, it was said, "is ninety-nine percent Proof against Influenza" and the "only known preventative."[23]

REFUSES TO DON INFLUENZA MASK; SHOT BY OFFICER

SAN FRANCISCO, Oct. 28.—While scores of passersby scurried for cover, H. D. Miller, a deputy health officer, shot and severely wounded James Wisser, a horseshoer, in front of a downtown drug store early today, following Wisser's refusal to don an influenza mask.

According to the police, Miller shot in the air when Wisser first refused his request. Wisser closed in on him and in the succeeding affray was shot in the arm and the leg.

Wisser was taken to the central emergency hospital, where he was placed under arrest for failure to comply with Miller's order.

TOP: The *Bellingham Herald* reported on the sometimes deadly consequences—not just from exposure but from aggressive law enforcement—of not donning a mask. (1918)

BOTTOM: The *Illustrated Current News* offered suggestions on how to prevent influenza. (1918)

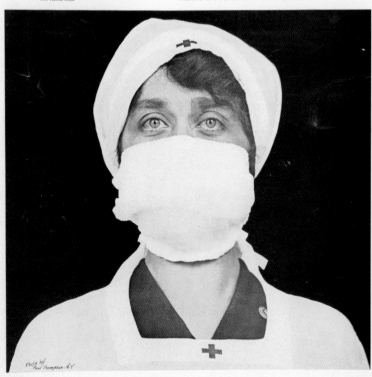

ILLUSTRATED CURRENT NEWS

Published 3 times a week. Subscription 40c per week. Illustrated Current News, Inc., 982 Chapel Street, New Haven, Conn.

Entered as second class matter October 20, 1915, at the Post Office at New Haven, Connecticut, under Act of March 3, 1879

Vol. 1   No. 788
October 18, 1918

To Prevent Influenza!

Do not take any person's breath.
Keep the mouth and teeth clean.
Avoid those that cough and sneeze.
Don't visit poorly ventilated places.
Keep warm, get fresh air and sunshine.
Don't use common drinking cups, towels, etc.
Cover your mouth when you cough and sneeze.
Avoid Worry, Fear and Fatigue.
Stay at home if you have a cold.
Walk to your work or office.
In sick rooms wear a gauze mask like in illustration.

Photo by Paul Thompson-N.Y.

Such statements were nonsense born of ignorance, fear, and hope. And also magical thinking, the notion that something happens just because we think about it or wish for it. But wish as people might, a gauze mask never shielded anyone from the flu virus. How could it? The virus is so tiny that loosely woven gauze has as much chance of intercepting it as a tennis racket has of snaring a speck of dust.

Other "prevention" methods were equally worthless. Some people—probably Republicans—urged, in all seriousness, voting Republican, "and you need have no fear of the flu." No, put sulfur in your shoes. No, pull out your teeth and tonsils. No, go about naked. The *New York Herald* quoted Boston physician Charles E. Page: "Influenza is caused chiefly by excessive clothing on an animal by nature naked. . . . [So] we need not wonder at the high death rate." The *Denver Post* urged readers to have "a clean mouth, a clean shirt and clean bowels" to avoid the disease. Finally, in Phoenix, Arizona, rumor had it that dogs carried influenza, so people shot their pets.[24]

Once people fell ill with influenza, as the best physicians knew, medical science could do nothing to cure them; curing lay in the hands of God and in their own immune systems. After the war, Dr. Herbert French, an English flu expert admired in America, was brutally frank. "No matter what treatment was adopted," he declared, "it was extremely difficult, if possible at all, to modify the course of the disease in the least. . . . One would be only too thankful if one knew anything which would with any certainty check the disease process, but one met nothing that was in the least degree successful in this respect."[25]

However, as in ancient times, physicians in 1918 felt duty-bound to try something—anything. Not a few declared a positive attitude a useful preventive. Dr. William C. Woodward, Boston's heath commissioner, advised people not to be afraid, because "fear would lower the vitality of those exposed to influenza." He failed to explain how seeing death all around could *not* frighten them. Other physicians held extreme, even crackpot, views. Despite their good intentions, they inflicted "treatments" that had no effect on the disease but actually weakened patients, increasing the odds against their survival. We need mention only a few to see what these were like.[26]

Physicians prescribed mustard plasters, an old-time remedy made of mustard-seed paste, to stimulate healing. When, for example, Abraham Lincoln was shot in 1865, his doctors covered the dying president's chest with mustard plasters. Influenza patients also received enemas of soapy water or warm milk. Some physicians thought it a good idea to rub goose grease on a patient's chest. Rupert Blue, the U.S. surgeon general, touted his favorite remedy:

Saturate a ball of cotton as large as a one-inch marble with spirits of alcohol. Add three drops of chloroform to each ball of cotton. Place it in between the patient's teeth. Let the patient inhale the fumes for 15 minutes, then rest 15 minutes, or longer, if needed. Then inhale again 15 minutes and repeat the operation as directed 24 times. The result will be that the lungs will expand to their normal condition.

Dr. Blue did not say if he used this treatment on real patients, let alone on his loved ones, or if they survived.[27]

As in plague-ravaged London in 1665, unscrupulous people tried to line their pockets. Until the 1930s, the United States had no laws to regulate patent medicines, drugs sold without a doctor's prescription. Makers of nonprescription medicines did not have to prove their products safe and effective, or list ingredients on the label, or have medical or scientific training. As a result, each year saw a fresh crop of drugs, many containing opium, a highly addictive

An advertisement for an influenza "miracle prevention." Like most, this atomizer would have been useless in combating the spread of the virus. (1918)

narcotic, for various ailments: stomach cramps, constipation, diarrhea, bed-wetting, fatigue, and "female monthly disorders."

The pandemic gave rise to scores of "miracle drugs." Newspapers carried ads for marvels: "Influ-BALM Prevents Spanish Flu," "Benetol, a powerful bulwark for the prevention and treatment of Spanish influenza." Another ad asked: "Sick with influenza? Use Ely's cream Balm. No more snuffling. No struggling for breath." A similar ad praised a competing drug: "Use Oil of Hyomi. Bathe your breathing organs with antiseptic balsam." Munyon's Paw Paw Pills guaranteed "influenza insurance." C. I. Hood & Company of Lowell, Massachusetts, offered three anti-influenza potions: Hood's Sarsaparilla, which, its ad boasted, was ideal for "impure, exhausted blood"; Hood's Pills, which would "regulate the bowels to a nicety"; and Hood's Pepitron (chocolate pills), which would fortify the entire body. Ads for Tanlac Reconstructive Tonic told the truth in one respect: "Influenza Claims More Victims Than German Bullets."[28]

Desperate people also turned to folk medicine, traditional remedies favored over generations within various societies. Often they put their faith in magical objects. Southern mountain folk, for example, kept shotguns under sickbeds to "draw out" the fever. Elsewhere, to ward off infection, people hung cloth bags filled with camphor around their necks, or they swallowed doses of red pepper, powdered asparagus, or "kerosene on sugar." Recipes called for wearing a necklace of chicken feathers or asafetida, also known as "devil's dung" an herb that "smelled like rotten flesh." The idea was that foul odors could chase influenza "germs" away. During outbreaks of the Black Death, Europeans had inhaled the stench from latrines for the same reason. Some Americans swore by the curative powers of onions. An Oregon woman boasted that she doused her sick four-year-old daughter with onion syrup and buried her from head to toe for three days in freshly cut, eye-watering onions. She said the child recovered—to the delight of onion growers.[29]

The clergy turned to prayer. Billy Sunday spoke for his colleagues of all faiths. At a prayer meeting in his

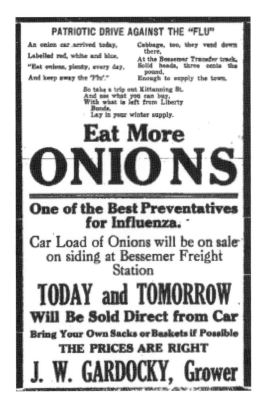

PATRIOTIC DRIVE AGAINST THE "FLU"

An onion car arrived today,   Cabbage, too, they vend down
Labelled red, white and blue,   there,
"Eat onions, plenty, every day,   At the Bessemer Transfer track,
And keep away the 'Flu'."   Solid heads, three cents the
                                     pound,
                                     Enough to supply the town.

So take a trip out Kittanning St.
And see what you can buy,
With what is left from Liberty
Bonds,
Lay in your winter supply.

Eat More
ONIONS

One of the Best Preventatives for Influenza.

Car Load of Onions will be on sale on siding at Bessemer Freight Station

TODAY and TOMORROW

Will Be Sold Direct from Car

Bring Your Own Sacks or Baskets if Possible

THE PRICES ARE RIGHT

J. W. GARDOCKY, Grower

Onions offered no protection against influenza—but ample opportunity for profit. (1918)

Providence, Rhode Island, tabernacle, Sunday mounted the speaker's platform brimming with confidence. After a moment's pause to survey the thousands of upturned faces, he threw his arms wide. "We can," he cried, "meet here tonight and pray down the epidemic just as well as we can pray down a German victory." We cannot say if this message reassured anybody. For as Sunday spoke, feverish members of the con-gregation collapsed and ushers carried them from the building.[30]

THE RANKS OF DEATH

The week of October 23, 1918, is unique in American history. Within seven days, influenza claimed 21,000 lives, still the highest number of deaths from any cause ever recorded in a week in this country. Not even the horror days of the Civil War were so deadly.[31]

On October 23, health department records show, 851 New Yorkers died of the disease, the highest daily figure ever recorded in the city, and for several days the death toll did not fall below 800. But in Philadelphia, the death toll that week was even worse: 5,270 people died in the "City of Brotherly Love"—more than 700 times above the normal death rate for all causes. Stunned Red Cross volunteers noted that daily death notices "fill an entire [newspaper] page, seven columns of small print with a repetitious litany: '. . . of pneumonia, age 21,' '. . . of influenza, age 26.' The toll is heaviest among young adults."[32]

Few Americans, then as now, had ever seen a person die, let alone

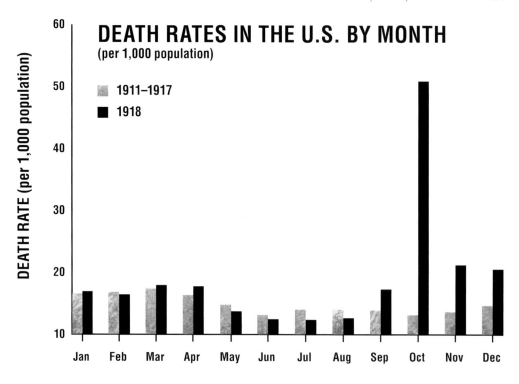

touched a corpse. This was not the case during the pandemic. Flu-ravaged cities seemed like the plague-torn London of 1665. Victims' bodies accumulated in beds and closets and odd corners of homes until corpse collectors took them away. In Philadelphia, the nation's worst-hit city, the police ordered families to leave their dead on their porches or on the sidewalks in front of their homes. Each body had to be wrapped in a bedsheet "for sanitary reasons."

As in Daniel Defoe's London, Philadelphia had so-called dead wagons. A survivor recalled, "An open truck came through the neighborhoods and picked up the bodies." Families took this hard—very hard. "It was just too much to bear, having to put your loved one on the street for a truck to take them away," said Harriet Ferrell. In normal times, residents put their trash barrels on the curb for sanitation workers to pick up.[33]

The dead wagons rumbled through backstreets, stopping only to allow volunteers to collect bodies. Selma Epp lost her brother Daniel. "My aunt," the Philadelphian remembered years later, "saw the horse-drawn wagon coming down the street. The strongest person in our family carried Daniel's body to the sidewalk. Everyone was too weak to protest. There were no coffins in the wagon, just bodies piled on top of each other. Daniel was two; he was just a little boy. They put his body in the wagon and took him away."[34]

There were so many bodies that coffins became scarce nearly everywhere. As demand rose, "coffin ghouls"—greedy manufacturers—jacked up prices, even to $500, as much as poor families earned in a year. Desperate people did desperate things to give loved ones a decent burial. "We had caskets stacked up outside the funeral home," an undertaker said. "We had to have guards kept on them because people were stealing the caskets." In Germany, by contrast, families had to rent coffins for funerals and then return them empty at the end of the day. Poor Japanese families fashioned coffins from wooden barrels, cardboard, and paper.[35]

American funerals were often anything but "proper." Many gravediggers were themselves ill with flu, or were terrified of it, forcing the deceased's family to take over. "It was either that or they weren't going to get the grave open," a man recalled. On especially busy days in Philadelphia, the Bureau of Highways used a steam shovel to dig trenches in which to bury the poor. In Norway, where the ground froze deep in winter, families hung their dead in trees until the spring thaw.[36]

To make matters worse, American officials often placed limits on the number of mourners who could attend a funeral and how long it might last. Chicago health authorities ruled: "No one except adult relatives and friends not to exceed 10 persons in addition to the undertaker, undertaker's assistants, minister and necessary drivers shall be permitted to attend any funeral." No exceptions allowed, so don't ask.[37]

Influenza was an equal opportunity killer. It was no respecter of sex or race, education or wealth; anyone was a potential victim. Newspapers carried weekly lists titled "Prominent People Who Have Died of Influenza." Among these were athlete George Freeth Jr., the "Father of Modern Surfing"; writer Randolph Bourne; composer Charles Tomlin-

Almost 4,000 people died in Boston as a result of the flu epidemic of 1918 during its first weeks.

BOSTON DEATH RECORD AS RESULT OF EPIDEMIC

	Influenza	Pneumonia	Total
Sept 14	9	12	21
Sept 15	15	9	24
Sept 16	23	5	28
Sept 17	28	13	41
Sept 18	30	13	43
Sept 19	32	10	42
Sept 20	44	10	54
Sept 21	57	23	80
Sept 22	44	19	63
Sept 23	74	13	87
Sept 24	81	28	109
Sept 25	81	24	105
Sept 26	123	33	156
Sept 27	107	37	144
Sept 28	128	24	152
Sept 29	119	30	149
Sept 30	142	29	171
Oct 1	152	50	202
Oct 2	135	40	175
Oct 3	166	25	191
Oct 4	154	29	183
Oct 5	117	32	149
Oct 6	153	37	190
Oct 7	146	24	170
Oct 8	123	27	150
Oct 9	124	20	144
Oct 10	96	28	124
Oct 11	103	18	121
Oct 12	94	27	121
Oct 13	72	13	85
Oct 14	94	25	119
Oct 15	67	31	98
Oct 16	57	14	71
Oct 17	41	12	53
Oct 18	44	16	60
Totals	3075	800	3875

son Griffes; silent film actor Harold Lockwood; and educator Ella Flagg Young. Survivors included cartoonist Walt Disney, painter Georgia O'Keeffe, silent-film star Mary Pickford, and Pulitzer Prize–winning author Katherine Anne Porter. *Pale Horse, Pale Rider,* Porter's account of her illness told in the form of a novel, is at once sensitive and chilling.[38]

Assistant Secretary of the Navy Franklin D. Roosevelt had a close shave. FDR, as everyone called him, had gone to France in September to inspect U.S. bases. Though he stayed in a top Paris hotel, he could not escape the fact that influenza made Parisians sad and nervous. On the return voyage from Brest, he fell critically ill with the flu, but he survived. Had he died in 1918, it would have changed the course of world history. Elected president in 1932, FDR saw America through its worst economic crisis, the Great Depression, as well as the Second World War.

The pandemic harmed the U.S. economy. High absenteeism affected every industry. Miners' illnesses and deaths cut coal production by half in certain areas. In Pennsylvania, production in a major mine fell from 1,100 tons to 200 tons a day. Such a shock to coal supplies had the same impact as a severe oil shortage would today. Coal powered the steam engines that drove factory machines.

Influenza and coal shortages hit the steel industry, which made the metal used for everything from safety pins to battleships. Ford Motor Company, the world's leading manufacturer of cars and trucks, had steel shortages and over 2,000 workers down with flu at its plants in Detroit. Despite heroic efforts, munitions factories were forced to reduce their output of bullets and artillery shells. Philadelphia's shipyard at Hog Island, the world's largest, delayed production and repairs because of the lack of steel and its flu-reduced workforce.[39]

Federal, state, and local governments limped along as best they could. In Washington, D.C., flu struck suddenly and killed swiftly. One afternoon, a young woman called an emergency number about her three roommates. Two were dead and one was dying, so could someone please come? She herself felt perfectly fine. Shortly afterward, the police arrived and found four bodies. Influenza also felled hundreds of police officers and firefighters, raising fears that the nation's capital would dissolve in chaos. This possibility gave the fire chief nightmares. "The whole city'd burn to the ground if a fire ever got started," he groaned. Every government department had

FLU EPIDEMIC

It almost stopped the works in 1918!

A cartoon depicting influenza's devastating impact on American manufacturing. (1918)

to make do without key people. Flu even forced the U.S. Supreme Court to adjourn. Justice Oliver Wendell Holmes called its quarters in the Capitol "this crowded and infected place." In courts across the nation, jurors rebelled, refusing to stay together in the same room.[40]

AMERICA'S CHILDREN

Influenza robbed countless youngsters of normal childhoods. For them, attending school had been a regular part of life. The pandemic, however, forced local authorities to decide whether to keep public schools open; private schools decided this for themselves. Most officials played it safe, ordering district schools closed for a few days, weeks, or months. Yet three major cities—New York, Chicago, and New Haven, Connecticut—kept their public schools open throughout the pandemic. Their reasons for doing so were much the same; we will focus on New York because it had the nation's largest number of pupils.[41]

The city's schools served nearly one million children, of whom three out of four lived in crowded, rundown tenements. At first, health of-

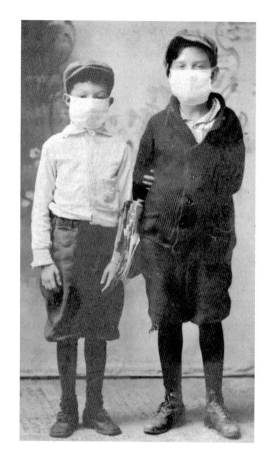

Children ready for school during the 1918 flu pandemic.

ficials wanted to follow the rest of the country, closing schools until the crisis passed. However, Dr. Sara Josephine Baker (1873–1945), head of the Bureau of Child Hygiene, argued for keeping them open. She asked the health commissioner, Dr. Royal S. Copeland, a simple question: "If you have a system where you could examine one-fifth of the population of

Sara Josephine Baker, an American physician notable for making contributions to public health, especially among the immigrant communities of New York City. (1925)

the city every morning, and control every person who showed any symptom of influenza, what would it be worth to you?" Startled by Baker's question, Copeland replied, "Well, that would be almost priceless." Like Baker, he decided "children are better off in school, under supervision, than playing about in the streets." New York's public schools stayed open.[42]

Baker was a bundle of energy. Thanks to her wit and will, schools became havens from influenza. They already offered a clean environment, visited by doctors and nurses for routine medical inspections. Now children were forbidden to gather outside before the school day began. Instead, monitors hurried them straight to their classrooms, where teachers checked for telltale symptoms: runny noses, red eyes, sneezing, coughing. Children with any of these symptoms were immediately sent to the nurse's office for further examination. A school secretary took a sick child either home to be put to bed or directly to a hospital emergency room. Schools also emphasized good hygiene as a way to prevent disease. As for influenza, each class had to have its "Daily Gargle"—cleansing mouths and throats with salt water as the eagle-eyed teacher looked on.[43] (Gargling, however, is useless against flu viruses.)

Baker's program was an amazing success. It had beaten the odds. When the pandemic finally passed, Dr. Copeland reported: "The number of cases of influenza among children of school age was so small as to be negligible. There was no evidence at all, in this age group [six to fifteen], that there had been any

epidemic of influenza in the city." New York's children were lucky— mostly. Elsewhere, things were decidedly different.[44]

For young survivors of the pandemic, life would never be the same. Like shell-shocked soldiers, they bore emotional scars.

These children had similar experiences and shared similar feelings—of anxiety, of terror, of despair. Parents could not hide their own feelings, try as they might. Youngsters might not know exactly what was happening, but parents could not help sending nonverbal signals. "I knew my par-

ents were worried," recalled William Maxwell of Lincoln, Illinois, who later became an editor at the *New Yorker* magazine. "I paid less attention to their words than to the sound of their voices. When they discussed it, I heard anxiety."[45]

Fear became so strong that one could almost touch it. For Bill Sardo, son of a Washington, D.C., funeral director, fear was a living presence. "From the moment I got up in the morning to when I went to bed at night, I felt a constant sense of fear," he recalled as an adult. "We were afraid to kiss each other, to eat with each other, to have contact of any kind.... Fear tore people apart." Don Tonkel of Goldsboro, North Carolina, said, "[I] felt like I was walking on eggshells.... I remember I was actually afraid to breathe. People were afraid to talk to each other. It was like—don't breathe in my face, don't even look at me, because you might have the germs that will kill me."[46]

There was plenty to be afraid of. Death seemed to lurk everywhere. Kenneth Crotty of Framingham, Massachusetts, was eleven when the "great flu" reached his block. "It was scary," he said years later, "because every morning when you got up, you asked, 'Who died during the night?' You know death was there all the time." In New Haven, Connecticut, John Delano knocked every morning on the door of his friends' house, but no one ever answered. Finally, John's mother told him that "God had taken them. My friends had gone to Heaven."[47]

Terrible experiences forced some youngsters to mature quickly. Francis Russell, later an author and journalist, was seven years old when the pandemic struck. The boy lived with his family on top of Dorchester Hill, from which he could see Boston and the troopships in Boston Harbor. To support the war effort, Francis bought thrift stamps at twenty-five cents each, and he ate peaches to save the pits, which were made into charcoal for gas masks. Every day, too, he watched funeral processions pass by and saw coffins pile up under a large tent at a local cemetery. Francis and two friends became curious. What, exactly, happened to those coffins? they wondered. One day they sneaked into the cemetery, hid on the slope of a low hill, and watched a funeral in progress. A gravedigger saw them and chased them away.

It was getting dark, and as Francis walked home alone, he had a sudden insight—one that changed the way he saw the world. For the first time, the youngster became aware of time. Not the time to go to bed or to wake up or to eat, but the eternal rush of time. It left him shaken, but wise beyond his years. He explained later: "I knew then that life was not a perpetual present, and that even tomorrow would be part of the past, and that for all the days and years to come, I too must one day die. I pushed the relentless thought aside, knowing even as I did so that I should never again be wholly free of it." Whoever they were, whatever they wished, mortal humans shared the same fate.[48]

Many children had to grow up faster than Francis Russell, whose parents survived. When a father, the family's breadwinner, died, someone had to put food on the table. Often widows did double duty as mothers and breadwinners. If they could not, their children had to go to work. Melvin Frank, for example, was stunned when influenza took his father. The loss sent him "reeling," he said. "My world had tumbled in." Suddenly, at age twelve, he became "the man of the family." A week after his father's funeral, Melvin found a job, his childhood and school days over.[49]

Losing one's mother could be an even worse blow. The devil virus was especially adept at killing pregnant women. Mattie Varner, a midwife in Atlanta, Georgia, felt helpless because her clients "were dying just like leaves off them trees." Varner did not exaggerate. Among mothers-to-be, as many as 71 percent of those

infected by the virus died. Some died while giving birth to live babies; others miscarried or delivered dead infants.[50]

Young children had great difficulty coping with a mother's loss. When William Maxwell was ten, influenza took his mother, and he discovered he was living in a dangerous world. "The shine went out of everything," he later told an interviewer. "I realized, for the first time and forever, that we were not safe. We were not beyond harm."[51]

Yet Maxwell was lucky; he still had his father. Orphans had no parents. Some became homeless, surviving by their wits and luck. In Minneapolis, Minnesota, police officers found a hundred children, some sick, all malnourished, living on the streets. Many wound up in orphanages, though a few were adopted or placed in foster homes. Families also passed orphans from relative to relative. Mary McCarthy, later a famous writer, was six when influenza claimed both her parents. Though taken in by a wealthy aunt, she and her three younger brothers felt scorned and deserted, unwanted and helpless. "It was thought," she recalled bitterly, "that we should know we were orphans and fitted for a different destiny than our well-tended cousins."[52]

HEROES, HEROINES, AND ORDINARY FOLKS

As a young Mary McCarthy learned, the pandemic showed men and women at their worst and at their best. A person's basic character did not change under its pressure. Faced with such horror, people revealed their real selves, only in exaggerated form. The selfish became more selfish. The callous remained cold-hearted. The cowardly gave in to hysteria, cringed, and whined in self-pity. The brave and dutiful, by their actions, became almost holy.

There was enough selfishness and cowardice to go around. "Not one of the neighbors would come in and help," a survivor recalled. Sometimes landlords evicted tenants just because they were unlucky enough to have the flu. Cowardice, however, might also have a silver lining. Despite the ability to hide their identity by wearing gauze masks, Chicago muggers

feared flu more than they feared jail. One young woman calmly walked home from her job late at night; if a stranger approached, she began coughing violently.[53]

More often than not, however, Americans tried to help each other. This was especially true within the medical profession. As in wartime Europe, the needs of the military came first. When Congress declared war on Germany in April 1917, just 776 out of America's 140,000 physicians were serving in the armed forces. When the war ended in November 1918, more than 38,000 of them had enlisted.[54]

A civilian public health official described the wartime doctor shortage: "There were sections of the country that were absolutely stripped of physicians." Frantic officials in state capitals tried to fill the gaps any way they could. Calls went out to nursing homes for retired physicians to volunteer during the emergency. One old-timer was eighty-five years old, another had a wooden leg, and another had a drug addiction. Medical students left their lecture halls for hospital wards. In addition, 173 New

Orleans dentists volunteered, though the devil virus never attacked teeth.[55]

Physicians did the best they could, given what they knew about influenza, which was next to nothing. Day in and day out, they worked under terrific pressure. Patients cried, "Doctor! Doctor! Do something, give us something, Doctor!" But doctors had nothing useful to give, except massive doses of aspirin.[56]

Despite their hard work, physicians had little to show for their efforts. Their frustration grew, and with it anguish. In the small Arkansas town of Central, for instance, Lillie Ladd remembered how a visiting doctor broke down in front of her husband, Melvin. The doctor was exhausted and could offer no hope to a stricken family member. "This is my twenty-fifth case," he groaned, "and I've lost the first twenty-four." Besides, physicians were human beings, not gods. For many weeks, the *Journal of the American Medical Association* printed page after page of short obituaries, in small type, of doctors who died of influenza.[57]

The disease put American hospitals under severe strain, too. The flood of patients used up supplies faster than they could be replaced. Across the country, hospitals reported shortages of basic items: gowns, pajamas, slippers, gauze masks, towels, blankets, sheets, and pillowcases. Flu patients occupied many, if not most, hospital beds. Things got so bad in New York's Bellevue Hospital that nurses put three to a bed in the children's ward. At another hospital, a nurse, Carla Morrissey, recalled walking into a forty-one-bed ward. She described conditions like those my father found in Siberia when he came down with influenza. Not only were all the beds occupied, "but there were boys laying on the floors and on the stretchers waiting for that boy in a bed to die."[58]

Nurses were in greater demand than doctors. When authorities in Bath, Maine, telegraphed a Boston hospital pleading for two doctors, the return message read: "Can send all the doctors you want but not one nurse."[59]

At first glance, this seems not to make sense; after all, doctors had to study for years and pass rigorous examinations before getting their licenses to practice medicine. However, despite all their knowledge,

WANTED
25000 STUDENT NURSES

U.S. STUDENT NURSE RESERVE

ENROLL AT THE NEAREST RECRUITING STATION OF THE WOMANS COMMITTEE OF THE COUNCIL OF NATIONAL DEFENSE

A recruitment poster seeking student nurses. Because of their ability to provide "tender loving care" as well as perform administrative duties, nurses were often in higher demand than doctors during the pandemic. (c. 1917-1919)

they knew nothing of the true cause of influenza, much less how to cure it. Ditto for nurses. But nurses provided vital supportive care; they called it TLC—tender loving care. Nurses did the hundreds of small things, from fluffing pillows to speaking calmly, that made patients comfortable, hopefully keeping them alive until the infection passed. TLC,

as historian Alfred W. Crosby rightly says, "was the miracle drug of 1918."[60]

Until the mid-1800s, nurses were considered ignorant people unfit for any other type of work. Often they were "fallen women," sinners whom judges asked to choose between nursing and jail. This negative view changed thanks to the pioneering work of Florence Nightingale in England and Clara Barton, founder of the American Red Cross. Both trained "lady nurses," demanding knowledge, efficiency, "good character," and "sound morals." By 1918, nursing had come into its own as a profession.

When the United States joined the Allies, it had 98,162 highly trained "graduate nurses." Of these, roughly 16,000 would enlist, serving at army camps at home and with the AEF in France.[61]

Civilian nurses worked every bit as hard as their military sisters. The pandemic became the supreme test of their ability and character. Routinely, big-city nurses worked twelve-hour shifts in flu wards. One, Dorothy Deming, described a typical shift in New York's Presbyterian Hospital: "Almost overnight the hospital was

Red Cross volunteers assisting during the epidemic. (1918)

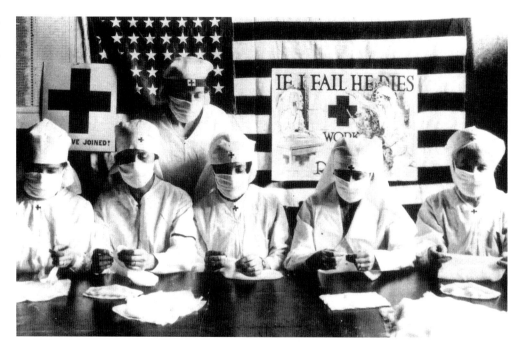

inundated.... Wards emptied hastily of patients convalescing from other ailments ... and only emergency operations were performed. Cots appeared down the center of wards.... Victims came on stretchers ... their faces and nails as blue as huckleberries."[62]

Constant emotional stress got the best of even the strong-willed. One night Dorothy Deming and another nurse, also named Dorothy, lost their battle to save a flu patient. Come morning, they broke the heart-wrenching news to the patient's family. Crying inwardly, Deming tried

to hide her feelings. She rushed to a linen closet, "always our place of refuge, and there ahead of me, was Dorothy sobbing her heart out. We really let go. I wonder about this sometimes when I hear people say nurses are hard-boiled."[63]

When things got really bad, nurses worked extra shifts. Though groggy from lack of sleep, they forced themselves to stay focused, braced by mugs of steaming black coffee. Like doctors, they got the flu, and some died of it. At one point, Minneapolis's City Hospital reported nearly half its nursing staff had been down with influenza during a three-week period. At New York's Mount Sinai Hospital, eighty-five nurses fell ill, of whom eighteen developed pneumonia. Yet when the student nurses were ordered to remain home until the danger passed, "the class voted unanimously to stay and serve."[64]

Despite all the hardships, many nurses said they would not have traded their experiences for anything. "For me, nursing came alive during that test," Dorothy Deming wrote in 1957. "Now, patients came first. Reassure them, ease them, help them, watch them . . . and comfort them. . . . This was nursing as I had dreamed of it; it was nursing at its most demanding. . . . We grew to full professional stature in those dark days."[65]

Deming and her sisters were not alone. The nurse shortage challenged other women eager to show their ability and patriotism. The American Red Cross helped mobilize them in the fight against influenza. A flyer pleaded:

Red Cross nurses during a demonstration at a Red Cross Emergency Ambulance Station. (1918)

A STERN TASK FOR STERN WOMEN

There is nothing in the epidemic of SPANISH INFLUENZA to inspire panic.

There is everything to inspire coolness and courage and sacrifice on the part of American women.

A stern task confronts our women—not only trained women, but untrained women. . . .

HUMANITY CALLS UPON THEM

LIVES DEPEND ON THEIR
ANSWER. . . .

WILL YOU ENROLL FOR
SERVICE NOW?[66]

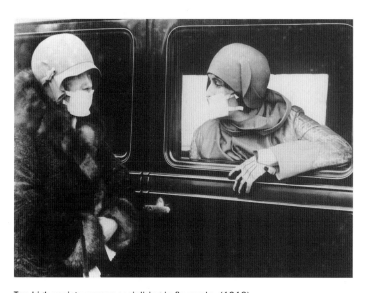

Two high-society women socializing in flu masks. (1918)

They enrolled. New York society women—the mothers, wives, and daughters of America's richest men—heard the call. Lillian Wald, founder of the Henry Street Settlement, which provided the first visiting nurse service in the United States, saw them in action. "Dignified and discerning women," Wald noted, "stood on the steps of Altman's and Tiffany's Fifth Avenue shops and accosted passers-by." Volunteers, the fur-clad and bejeweled ladies declared, needed only "willingness and courage" to serve.[67]

Franklin D. Roosevelt's wife, Eleanor, overcame her fears to work in a Red Cross canteen, where she served hot meals to troops bound for France. The wife of William Randolph Hearst, America's most influential newspaper owner, answered the call to help. She and her society friends sped across New York City in their limousines as members of "flying squads." Other women worked in hospitals, bringing patients food, carrying stretchers, and cleaning. They also rubbed shoulders with lower-class volunteers from the tenements. A Wald aide recalled that one tireless worker "who could always be counted on" had been a prostitute.[68]

Helping others did wonders for volunteers' self-esteem. Why, if women showed such dedication and courage in this crisis, they could do anything—even vote in elections! Opponents argued that "the ladies" should not have the right to vote because they were too unstable, too emotional, too "fragile" to make important decisions without male guidance. Women's activities during the pandemic helped change minds.

Thus, it was no accident that, in August 1920, most states approved the Nineteenth Amendment to the U.S. Constitution, which granted women the right to vote.

But in the fall of 1918, nobody could predict the future. Big questions preyed on people's minds. Would the Allied or the German home front crack first? Could the Americans, newcomers to the war, turn the tide of battle for the Allies? Whatever happened, one thing was sure: the devil virus would have its say.

The St. Louis Red Cross Motor Corps on duty, with stretchers at the ready. (1918)

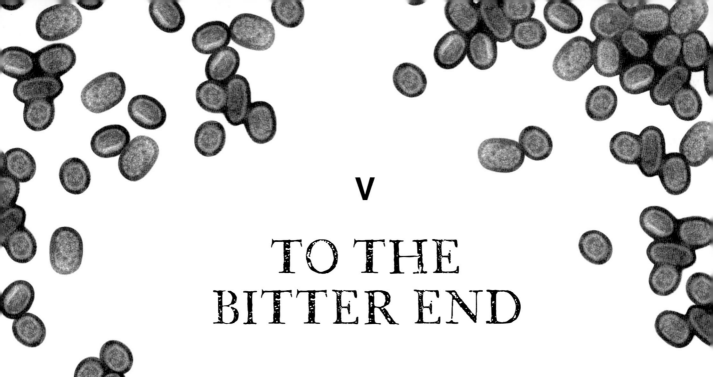

V

TO THE BITTER END

We can't stop this war on account of Spanish or any other kind of influenza.
—Colonel S. M. Kennedy, chief surgeon of the Port of New York,
August 18, 1918

THE BIG PUSH

On a rainy afternoon late in August 1918, Allied commanders, elegant in their spotless uniforms and glistening black boots, stood before a wall map at French headquarters outside Paris. While the enemy still held huge chunks of France and Belgium, all signs pointed in the right direction: Germany was getting weaker. General Ludendorff's spring offensive had failed, due in part to the first wave of the flu pandemic, which had since died out. Meanwhile, the Allies were gaining numerical superiority; more than 1.2 million American troops had arrived in France or were on the way. Now that the balance of forces had tipped in their favor, the commanders planned a massive attack on key points along the entire 550-mile Western Front. Its aim: to crush Germany's armies, leaving Germany no choice but to sue for peace on Allied terms.

The American commander, General John J. "Black Jack" Pershing (1860–1948), struck first, followed by the British, French, and Belgians in turn. On September 12, units from his First Army broke through the German lines at Saint-Mihiel, a strategic town on the Meuse River in northern France. On September 26, Pershing launched the Meuse-Argonne offensive, which would continue until November 11, the last day of the war. The offensive took its name from a twenty-one-mile stretch of the Western Front running eastward from the Meuse River near the fortress of Verdun to the western edge of the Argonne Forest. This was the largest American military operation since the Civil War. With the 1.5 million troops under his command, coupled with their modern weapons, Black Jack could easily have wiped out the combined Union and Confederate armies.[1]

At precisely 1:00 a.m., Pershing's artillery roared in unison, the weapons creating a false dawn with their gun flashes. The waiting AEF troops held their hands over their ears against the shattering noise. Men filing past the guns felt the hot breath

General John J. Pershing. (1917)

on their faces. It was, said medical officer William Holmes Dyer, "*the most* terrific bombardment of the war. . . . The old woods in which we were trembled as if by earthquake . . . and our ears were deafened." By early November, the U.S. army had fired off more artillery ammunition than the Union army had used in the entire four years of the Civil War.[2]

The German army resisted with every ounce of skill gained during four years of grueling combat. Dr. George Washington Crile, an American surgeon, noted the results in his diary on October 17: "Everything is overflowing with patients.

U.S. soldiers of the Twenty-Third Infantry, Second Division, firing a machine gun at a German position in the Argonne Forest, in France. (1918)

Our divisions are being shot up; the wards are full of machine-gun wounds. . . . Rain, rain; mud, blood; blood, death! All day, all night, we hear the incessant tramp of troops— troops going in, wounded coming back. Even in our dreams we hear it."[3]

German bombers attacked some hospitals near the front line nearly every night. Shirley Millard and other off-duty nurses slept in tents a few hundred yards from their hospital. After one ferocious air raid, Millard told her diary about "the blood red sky at sunrise." A tree next to the hospital "blossomed horribly with fragments of human bodies, arms and legs, bits of bedding, furniture, and hospital equipment." These "decorations" were like those for a devil's Christmas tree.[4]

Ambulances brought hundreds of poison-gas cases to Millard's hospital each day. The poor fellows, mostly boys away from home for the first time, "cannot breathe lying down or sitting up," Millard wrote. "They just struggle for breath. But nothing can be done. Their lungs were gone. . . . One boy, today, screaming to die. The entire top layer of his skin burned from his face and body." She gave him an injection of morphine, a drug made from opium, to dull his pain until the end came. She could not decide which was more ghastly: death by poison gas or by influenza. Often the two went hand in hand. Owing to their damaged lungs, gas victims were at greater risk of dying of the bacterial pneumonia that often went along with the flu.[5]

Unfortunately, the pandemic's second wave, its most lethal phase, coincided with the Meuse-Argonne offensive. Boston, New York, and Philadelphia were already struggling with its effects on civilians. Now the flu had "engulfed the First Army," its chief surgeon, Alexander N. Stark, told his superiors. General Pershing agreed; flu had laid him low for a few days. The disease, he reported on October 5, had "assumed serious proportions." By that date, army hospitals had nearly 70,000 flu patients, "of whom many developed a grave form of pneumonia"; 32 percent would die. In other words, these trained fighters lay helpless in bed instead of engaging the enemy.[6]

Reports poured into Pershing's

Nurses in gas masks tending to soldiers on the front line. (1917)

headquarters from front-line units telling of men who "could hardly drag themselves around," so sick had the flu made them. Yet the virus did more than eat into a soldier's body; it ate into his spirit. As letters from home brought news of the pandemic, soldiers worried about their loved ones.[7]

Captain Harry S. Truman, later the thirty-third president of the United States, served in an artillery unit during the Meuse-Argonne offensive. Truman's reaction reflected that of his comrades. Upon learning that the flu had struck his hometown of Independence, Missouri, the captain became frantic. His fiancée, Bess Wallace, and her brother Frank and two close friends had come down

A postcard photo taken in France of Harry S. Truman in his World War I uniform. (1918)

with the disease. Now the front, with all its dangers, seemed safer than the United States. Truman wrote: "Every day someone in my outfit will hear that his mother, sister, or sweetheart is dead. It is heartbreaking almost to think . . . that the ones we'd like to protect more than all the world would have been more exposed to death than we."[8]

Flu cases clogged the AEF's medical services. There were so many that medical personnel—stretcher bearers, ambulance drivers, field-hospital aides—had orders to separate flu cases from the wounded. But more often than not, this wasn't feasible—dodging enemy artillery shells and machine-gun bullets left no time to make a medical diagnosis. So they put all sorts of cases together, helter-skelter, exposing the wounded to infection. A flu-infected soldier, however, was more of a liability than a wounded soldier, because nobody else could "catch" a bullet wound. Thus, influenza killed wounded men who might otherwise have lived if they had been separated from their infected comrades and treated in time.[9]

Meanwhile, hospital staffs fought to save their patients, often a losing battle. Like their sisters back home, AEF nurses worked under intense pressure. "Patients have been pouring in with *grippe*," one wrote. "Work is desperate. A twelve-hour day with twenty minutes for lunch. . . . I think twenty-two patients have died now." For another nurse, influenza seemed "to be some frightful plague . . . and the proportion of deaths [is] higher—much higher—than we'd had for wounds at any time."[10]

In every army, nurses were the ones most beloved. They, more than any other medical professionals, carried the daily burden of caring for the sick and wounded. German soldiers worshiped *die Schwestern,* the sisters. To Allied soldiers, nurses were the "Roses of No Man's Land," beautiful flowers blooming amid the horrors. A sentimental song of the same title expressed their feelings:

> There's a Rose that grows in No
>   Man's Land,
> And it's wonderful to see.
> Tho' it's sprayed with tears,
> It will live for years
> In my garden of memory.
>
> It's the one red rose
> The soldier knows,
> It's the work of the Master's
>   Hand;
> In the War's great curse, stands
>   the Red Cross Nurse,
> She's the Rose of No Man's
>   Land.[11]

German nurses faced overwhelming odds at the front and at home. Their country suffered a lot worse than the Allies. Since German industry absorbed a large proportion of the workforce, including farmers, the nation depended on food

Sheet-music cover art for the ballad "The Rose of No Man's Land." (1918)

imported from abroad. This was a serious weakness, one that Britain, the world's leading naval power, was quick to exploit. By 1918, the Royal Navy's blockade had cut Germany off from all foreign sources of food, raw materials, medicines, and fertilizers. Put simply, the blockade aimed to create mass starvation. Winston Churchill, the civilian head of the Royal Navy, admitted its purpose was "to starve the whole population—men, women, and children, old and young, wounded and sound—into submission."[12]

Allied troops ate well; hungry Germans often raided their trenches to grab any food they found lying around. Equally important, since the Americans came, there were enough Allied soldiers to allow units to rest for a few days in the rear before returning to the trenches. Food shortages and exhaustion ravaged General Ludendorff's front-line troops, making them more vulnerable to influenza. "A tired man," Ludendorff correctly noted, "succumbs to contagion more easily than a vigorous man."[13]

German troops, too, worried about their families back in the "Fatherland." Conditions on the German home front worsened by the day. Owing to the blockade, shops had little or nothing to sell. Products made of rubber, cotton, and leather vanished from shelves. Soap grew scarce, so people and clothing stank. Once-prosperous citizens looked like tramps, dressed in dirty, threadbare clothes and shoes coming apart at the seams. Coal and electricity shortages made it impossible to heat homes. People froze to death in their beds. Hospitals ran out of medicines and gauze bandages; white paper substituted for bandages.

Yet food shortages took the greatest toll on civilian health and morale. German women "worn away to skin and bone, with seamed and careworn faces," roamed city streets searching for food, a medical officer reported. The government could only supply "war bread," a vile blend of turnips, potato skins, and sawdust. Hungry people ate stray cats, and rats, too. In Berlin, housewives butchered weakened and dead horses in the streets. "They fought each other for the best pieces, their faces and clothing covered with blood," a newspaper reported. "Other emaciated figures rushed over and scooped up the warm blood with cups and napkins. Only when the horse was reduced to a skeleton did the scavengers disperse, anxiously clutching bits of flesh to their hollow breasts." Things got so bad that law-abiding citizens took matters into their own hands. In Berlin, crowds looted shops, prompting the government to call in combat troops to restore order.[14]

A looted shop after a food riot in Berlin. (1918)

Germany's youngest suffered worst. Starving mothers could not produce enough milk to breast-feed their infants. A few weeks after the war ended, Henry W. Nevinson, a well-known English journalist, saw the result in Cologne, a leading industrial city. He wrote: "Although I have seen many horrible things in the world, I have seen nothing so pitiful as these rows of babies feverish from want of food, exhausted by privation to the point that their little limbs were like slender wands, their expressions hopeless, and their faces full of pain."[15]

Influenza scythed through Germany's hungry, weakened, stressed-out civilians. "Influenza Everywhere," said the headline of a Berlin newspaper, to nobody's surprise. In that city, it carried away over 1,700 people in a single day, October 15. In Hamburg, Germany's second-largest city, flu sent a daily average of 400 people to the cemetery. "We are returning every day to the barbarism of the Middle Ages in every way," a resident sighed. "I am astonished that there are no religious fanatics nowadays to run through the streets, dressed in sackcloth and ashes, and calling on the people to repent their sins." The anonymous writer was remembering the flagellants who'd tramped the roads during the Black Death of the fourteenth century. Government experts calculated that 763,000 Germans died as a result of the "hunger blockade."[16]

Despite the hardships, the German army fought with the courage of desperation. But the handwriting was on the wall. If fighting continued at the same pace, its position would collapse along the entire Western Front.

RUSH RUSH RUSH RUSH

General Pershing drew the same conclusion. At this critical moment in the war, he realized, numbers counted more than ever. If the Allies could keep up the pressure, keep hammering away, Germany would have to give up, saving countless lives. Still, there was a problem. Influenza had taken down so many American troops that an army division could not keep attacking for more than a few days without replacements. These could come from only one source—training camps in the United States. So, on October 8, Pershing cabled the War Department in Washington: "RUSH RUSH RUSH RUSH."[17]

Pershing's cable arrived just as the pandemic's second wave was rolling full speed across America. Army reports told of soaring death rates at training camps like Camp Devens. From a medical standpoint, it made no sense to push more recruits into these incubators of disease. The army's acting surgeon general, Charles Richard, urged its chief of staff, General Peyton March, to cancel all draft calls. "Epidemic influenza has become a very serious menace," he told March, "and threatens . . . to exact a heavy toll on human life, before the disease has run its course throughout the country." At the surgeon general's urging, on October 7 the army canceled the monthly draft call for 142,000 men. But General March, a stern old soldier, refused to go any further. Recruits already in training, or aboard ships at sea, would proceed to France whatever the cost, he insisted.[18]

The following evening—just hours after General Pershing's cable arrived at the War Department— General March met with President Woodrow Wilson. The commander in chief came straight to the point. "General March," he said, "I have heard representations made to me, by men whose ability and patriotism are unquestioned, that I should stop the shipment of men to France until the epidemic of influenza is under control."[19]

In reply, the general explained his views by citing the brutal arithmetic of war. To save *many* lives, leaders must be prepared to sacrifice *some* lives. Obviously, March told the president, the surest way to defeat Germany was to send more American troops to France. It followed that "the shipment of troops should not be stopped for *any* cause." Doing otherwise would slow and probably halt the Meuse-Argonne offensive, wasting all the lives already lost in that effort.[20]

Holding back would also send the

The twenty-eighth president of the United States, Woodrow Wilson was in office from 1913 to 1921. (1919)

wrong psychological message. How might German military leaders react, March wondered, if they believed the Americans were so frightened of influenza that they refused to commit more men at this critical time? Yes, men, perhaps thousands, would die crossing the "Big Pond," the Atlantic Ocean. But they would be dying for a noble cause—liberty, a cause greater than any individual. "Every such soldier who has died [of influenza] just as surely played his part as his comrade who died in France," March concluded.[21]

American presidents are not paid to make easy decisions. Now President

Wilson had, in effect, to authorize the deaths of any number of soldiers; there was no way to avoid it. Grimly, he made a historic decision. Wilson agreed with March. The flow of replacements would continue without letup. March stood stiffly at attention, snapped a salute, and turned to leave. Then, from out of the blue, Wilson recited a jump-rope rhyme making the rounds in the nation's schoolyards:

I had a little bird
And its name was Enza.
I opened the door
And in flew Enza.[22]

As soldiers boarded troopships, which they called "death ships," medical officers gave each a quickie examination, ordering anyone with flu symptoms into quarantine. But the devil virus was a stealthy thing; you could have it in your body for a day or two yet have no obvious symptoms.

Once aboard, men were confined in cramped spaces belowdecks. "Assigned quarters on lower deck," Private Eugene Kennedy wrote, "the blackest, foulest, most congested hole that I ever set foot into." The sound of thumping engines and clanging metal rang in their ears, preventing restful sleep. Some felt as if the steel walls were closing in on them. They slept in bunks—actually heavy-duty wire baskets—stacked four high. In stormy weather, sailors closed the portholes and had to breathe and rebreathe the same stale air. In areas where German submarines prowled, the ship's captain ordered lights-out, leaving them in total darkness. (Security was a serious matter: in February 1918, a submarine had sunk the troopship *Tuscania* with 2,000 American soldiers aboard, drowning 267.) The vessel's ceaseless rocking and pitching made them seasick. Since most were landlubbers, people not used to being on ships, they "heaved their guts." Men vomited on the deck, on themselves, and on those in the bunks beneath them.[23]

When flu symptoms appeared, victims sneezed, coughed, and vomited, spreading the virus to their comrades. "I was so feverish," Private Franklin Martin wrote in his diary, "I was afraid I would ignite [my] clothing. I had a cough that tore my insides out when I could not suppress it." When the ship's sick bay had no more space, men burn-

The African American troops of New York's famous 369th Infantry arriving at Hoboken, New Jersey, at the end of the war, as did many returning troops.

ing with fever had to sleep outside, on the upper deck. Those who died received a burial at sea, following a short prayer by the chaplain. To this day, some flu victims remain nameless because the army neglected to give them dog tags.[24]

The worst death ship of all was the *Leviathan,* a former luxury liner and the world's largest passenger ship. The *Leviathan* left Hoboken, New Jersey, on September 29, a week before President Wilson decided to allow troopships to sail despite the pandemic. Even before the anchor was raised, hundreds aboard fell ill with influenza. Although they were left behind, the *Leviathan* still had a "fifty percent overload": 9,033 troops, 2,000 crewmen, 200 army nurses. By the second day, 700 troops were down with flu—and more than 2,000 by the voyage's end.[25]

Those aboard compared the *Leviathan* to a slaughterhouse. According to a physician's report:

The USS *Leviathan* in a dazzle camouflage pattern. The *Leviathan* was formerly the *Vaterland,* a German ship owned by the Hamburg America Line and seized by the U.S. government in 1917. (1918)

[The scenes] cannot be visualized by anyone who has not actually seen them. Pools of blood from severe nasal hemorrhages of many patients were scattered throughout the compartments, and the attendants were powerless to escape tracking through the mess, because of the narrow passages between the bunks. The decks became wet and slippery, groans and cries of the terrified added to the confusion of [those] clamoring for treatment, and altogether a true inferno reigned supreme.[26]

By the time the *Leviathan* docked at Brest on October 8, at least eighty soldiers and sailors had died. As the army nurses walked down the gangplank, they wept. They had seen too much horror and were bone-deep exhausted. "Surely," a naval officer observed, "they had earned a place in heaven." Still, the dying continued. Nearly a thousand sick men came ashore, of whom about a hundred would die (the exact number is uncertain). After a few days of rest, the seemingly healthy crowded aboard trains bound for the trenches. Some of these, of course, had the virus in them and spread it to the front-line troops. Luckily, most newcomers would see little if any action because the war was drawing to an end.[27]

VICTORY, PEACEMAKING, AND INFLUENZA

General Pershing was right: by keeping up the pressure, the Allies broke through the German trench lines at several strategic places; at one point, they cut a key supply line. The enemy gave ground steadily, leaving behind thousands of prisoners, men too hungry, too tired, or too flu-ridden to keep going. Since nothing could hold back the tide of defeat, Berlin asked for an armistice, a truce while diplomats worked out a peace treaty. The Allies agreed, but only if Germany would accept their terms. To get a cease-fire, Germany must withdraw its forces from Allied territory, disband its army, and surrender all major weapons: heavy machine guns, artillery, aircraft, warships. In effect, Germany had to put itself at the Allies' mercy. When German representatives at the peace talks protested the harsh terms, they were told the offensive and the starvation blockade would continue until they "saw reason."

On November 11, at 5:10 a.m., German officials signed the armistice in a French railroad car parked in a forest just behind the front lines. The document said the armistice would take effect at 11-11-11—the eleventh hour, of the eleventh day, of the eleventh month of the year 1918. At that instant, the guns would fall silent, ending what was then the bloodiest conflict in history. Almost immediately, cease-fire orders were sent to the opposing forces by tele-

Soldiers celebrating the armistice that ended World War I. (1918)

phone, telegraph, and radio. We can only call what followed an outburst of mass insanity.

Many soldiers, on both sides, wanted the "honor" of firing the last shot of the war. As wristwatches ticked off the final minutes, it seemed that every gun on the Western Front cut loose at once. The cannons "were so hot that the paint is rising from them in blisters," a soldier recalled. Another wrote: "The shelling was heavy and . . . it grew steadily worse. It seemed to me that every battery in the world was trying to burn up its guns." Men called this the "mad moment." And in that moment, more than 10,000 men, including 3,000

Americans, were killed or wounded for nothing.[28]

When the guns finally fell silent, the effect was deafening. Captain Harry Truman's battery had let loose with the rest. Afterward, Truman wrote, "it was so quiet it made me feel as if I'd suddenly been deprived of my ability to hear." Then, he added, "holy hell" broke loose. From the Swiss border to the English Channel, men shouted and cheered and tossed their helmets into the air. *"Finie la guerre!"*—"The war is over!"— French troops cried as they ran into No Man's Land. Germans stood up in their trenches, roaring the same

words in their language: *"Der Krieg ist aus!"* British veterans belted out a favorite song:

When this lousy war is over,
No more soldiering for me.
When I get my civvy clothes on,
Oh how happy I shall be.[29]

American troops, according to a newspaper account, let out a "roar of voices" as if someone had scored the crucial touchdown at a college football game. But the Germans seemed happiest of all. They joined in, until "the rolling plain was alive with cheering men, friends and enemy alike." Members of an American

On the front lines in France, men of the U.S. Sixty-Fourth Regiment, Seventh Infantry Division, celebrate the news of the armistice. (1918)

fighter-plane squadron spoke for all the survivors: "I've lived through the war!" and "We won't be shot at any more!"[30]

People on the home fronts greeted the armistice with mixed feelings. In London, a boisterous crowd gathered in Trafalgar Square. Strangers sang, hugged, kissed, and snake-danced all night. Wounded soldiers dressed in hospital blue rode atop open double-decker buses, singing and beating time on the sides with their artificial legs. In Paris, fireworks lit the sky. The bells of Notre-Dame Cathedral rang out, and crowds surged down the long Avenue des Champs-Élysées to the Arc de Triomphe. In New York, jubilant crowds paraded through Manhattan, led by brass bands and, in one place, by circus elephants.[31]

The festivities also had a somber side, one usually omitted from schoolbooks and popular histories. There was sadness—plenty of it. In Paris, a newspaper reporter saw "too many women shrouded in black for whom victory had come too late." Winston Churchill had a similar experience in London. On his way home from a meeting, he came upon an elderly woman sobbing quietly. "Is there anything I can do for you?" he asked. "Thank you, no," she replied. "I am crying, but I am happy, for now I know that all my three sons who have been killed in the war have not died in vain." Across the Big Pond, in New York, a wrinkled black man sat on the steps of City

A *Los Angeles Times* bulletin announcing the end of combat. (1918)

Hall, weeping. He explained that he had been born a slave in Virginia and now had two sons killed in France for the sake of the country that had set him free.[32]

Nevertheless, the devil virus had not taken a holiday. During armistice celebrations, a Parisian observed, "germs were freely exchanged." She was right. Vast crowds, and the hugging and kissing of strangers, made it easier for the virus to spread. Influenza cases surged in the week after Armistice Day. "We really are faced with a huge epidemic," a doctor at the Hôpital Sainte-Anne reported, "before which we feel quite powerless." Flu deaths in Britain reached 19,000, an all-time record for so short a period.[33]

Returning troops added fuel to the fire. Disbanded units, fresh from the trenches, marched through Berlin, compounding the German capital's heavy flu burden. In Allied countries, family parties to celebrate a victor's safe return allowed the infection rate to soar. When the *Leviathan* docked at Hoboken with 8,000 troops late in December, they brought more influenza with them. By then, delegates had started to gather in Paris for the peace conference. It began in January 1919 at the Palace of Versailles, located eleven miles southwest of the French capital.[34]

Woodrow Wilson, the first president to leave the United States while in office, was the hero of the hour. His country had helped save the day when things looked bleakest for the Allies. Cheering crowds, brass bands, and seas of American flags greeted him in Britain and France. People hailed Wilson as the "prophet of the world," a "saint," and "Godsent" to bring peace to humanity. A man of many achievements, before winning the White House in 1912 he had been a respected historian, president of Princeton University, and governor of New Jersey. Wilson was also a hard-driving reformer who thought the federal government had the duty to fix society's ills, guaranteeing a decent standard of living for all citizens.[35]

The president also had a less attractive side. Woodrow Wilson was smug, domineering, and self-righteous. Certain that he wanted only the best for everyone, he thought opponents not merely wrong but wicked. Former president Theodore Roosevelt thought him "insincere and cold-blooded." After meeting Wilson, Britain's King George V told his private secretary, "I could not bear him. An entirely cold, academical professor—an odious man."[36]

The president hoped to make the World War "the war to end war." To achieve this aim, he wanted to create the League of Nations, an organization of peace-loving nations that would check aggressors—by war, if necessary. He called the proposed league "the enterprise of Divine mercy, peace and good will."[37]

Allied leaders, however, did not think the Almighty had anything to do with their war aims. British prime minister David Lloyd George and French prime minister Georges "the Tiger" Clemenceau thought of the sacrifices their peoples had made to defeat Germany. They wanted to prevent Germany from ever waging war again. Moreover, they meant to punish Germany by seizing German colonies and making the nation pay for the damage its armies had done. "The Germans," said Lloyd George,

In the foreground, from left to right, Clemenceau, Wilson, and Lloyd George leaving the Palace of Versailles after signing the peace treaty. (June 28, 1919)

"are going to be squeezed, as a lemon is squeezed—until the pips squeak." Though the American president was in favor of punishment, he thought Germany should be treated fairly. The nation should not be made so resentful as to become an outlaw nation and a future threat to world peace.[38]

As the peace conference got under way, an invisible assassin stalked its meetings. A member of Wilson's delegation described the conference as a "fug of flu." By that, he meant it took place against a background of influenza. The disease still raged in Paris. In December 1918, it killed

1,500 Parisians. During the week of February 22, 1919, it killed a record 2,676 people in the city.[39]

"It is the most depressing atmosphere I have ever seen in Europe," an American diplomat wrote from Paris. "Everyone seems to have something the matter with them." Nearly every member of the British delegation sniffled, coughed, and ran a fever. Flu killed Sir Mark Sykes, who had led the effort to break up the Ottoman Empire, placing its Arab lands under British and French control. Those lands—Iraq, Syria, Lebanon, and Palestine—are still in turmoil.[40]

Lloyd George had recovered from the flu, and so had Clemenceau; the Frenchman's son, however, had died of it. The French prime minister thought the American leader weak and naive. When Wilson's aides asked Clemenceau to talk privately with the president, he refused. "Talk with Wilson!" Clemenceau growled. "How can I talk with a fellow who thinks himself the first man in two thousand years to know anything about peace on earth?"[41]

Wilson held firm, arguing for his views about the peace treaty and the League of Nations. On April 3, 1919, however, he began to cough violently. He developed severe diarrhea, and his temperature shot up to 103° F.

The devil virus knocked the president flat on his back at a critical stage in the negotiations. Wilson recovered within the week, but the disease left its mark. He was not the same man—and never would be. "Something queer was happening in his mind," his valet Irwin "Ike" Hoover wrote years later. Aides noted that the president "lacked his old quickness of grasp." Colonel Edward M. House, Wilson's chief adviser on foreign affairs, agreed. Also recently recovered from the flu, House thought his boss had become "thoroughly discouraged," losing his will to fight for his beliefs.[42]

The colonel was right. When Wilson rejoined the talks, Lloyd George and Clemenceau held the League of Nations hostage to the harsh peace terms they wished to impose on Germany. Wilson caved in, and Germany was forced to sign the humiliating Treaty of Versailles on June 28, 1919. By signing, Germany accepted sole blame for starting the war and promised to pay $32 billion, an astronomical sum, as reparations. Britain, France, and Japan seized Germany's overseas possessions.

Sadly for Woodrow Wilson, the Americans turned against the League of Nations. The public feared that membership in it might get the United States involved in another world war that began in Europe. So the country did not join, crippling the organization from the outset. (The league idea was reborn after the Second World War with the creation of the United Nations and, this time, the firm support of the United States.) Most Germans denounced the peace treaty as unjust, humiliating, and lacking any legal or moral standing. Among them was a veteran temporarily blinded by poison gas. When that veteran, Adolf Hitler, recovered, he vowed to avenge the Treaty of Versailles, "the peace of shame," even if it took a second world war to do so. But that is a subject for another book.[43]

THE THIRD WAVE

The summer of 1919 saw the pandemic begin to retreat everywhere. Physicians noted an abrupt drop in new cases. "It was like you'd flipped

a switch," an American wrote. Yet the devil virus was unpredictable. In many places, influenza seemed almost gone, only to flare up, retreat, and flare up again. The third wave had begun. Regardless, the trend was clear: flu was loosening its grip. By mid-1920, the pandemic was over.[44]

Why?

At the time—and also in writings decades later—the pandemic was said to have "run its course." However, that is not a scientific explanation. The phrase is really an evasion, a way of disguising ignorance of what brought the pandemic to an end. Nothing happens without a cause, and the third wave was no exception. Researchers today believe

The Council of Four at the Paris Peace Conference: (from left) Prime Minister David Lloyd George of Great Britain, Prime Minister Vittorio Orlando of Italy, Prime Minister Georges Clemenceau of France, and President Woodrow Wilson of the United States. (1919)

the pandemic ended for two reasons: one military and political, the other the nature of viruses.

First, the physical environment no longer favored the devil virus. True, armistice celebrations, followed by masses of troops returning home, led to a spike in flu cases. However, the coming of peace also emptied the unhealthy trenches, training camps, and military bases, such as the one at Étaples. What is more, the Treaty of Versailles enabled Germany to resume food imports, ending the famine and increasing people's ability to resist infections of all sorts.

Second, just as the human immune system can be too robust, triggering a fatal overreaction, viruses can be too virulent—too deadly. Viruses, we recall, are not alive; they exist on the border of life. They do not "want" to harm, let alone kill, those they invade; that would be committing "suicide." Viruses must reproduce and pass their genes to the next generation. This process involves a delicate balance between their ability to infect new victims and to harm them. If a mutation allows a virus to, say, bypass the human immune system, the

virus stands a better chance of reproducing. If, however, a mutation destroys the virus before it reaches new victims, the cycle is broken. That strain of the virus will disappear, and the pandemic it caused will end.

Moreover, the natural process that makes a virus deadly also makes future versions of it milder. Different viral strains, resulting from subsequent mutations, inevitably occur. The devil virus was most unstable, always changing its capabilities. A mutation that makes its effects milder increases its chances of reproducing because it does not kill its host. The 1918 strain of the devil virus was as lethal as it could get; it is hard to imagine it being any worse. Future mutations, then, were bound to make it milder, more like the strains that cause seasonal flu. In other words, it is likely that the milder third-wave virus replaced its deadlier second-wave ancestor. Yet this is not a one-way street, since further mutations can turn a virus back into a mass killer.[45]

The human immune system, too, undoubtedly helped end the 1918 pandemic. Nobody knows whether an infectious disease can wipe out the entire human race; this has never happened, or you would not be reading these words. If the 1918 pandemic is any guide, humankind survived the worst disease event ever. Though exposed to the devil virus, the vast majority of people did *not* get sick, and those who did, survived. Having killed the most vulnerable—the very young, the very old, young adults, pregnant women—the virus must have run out of likely victims to infect.

To put it another way, the pandemic behaved like an immense forest fire: it eventually burned out. In nature, forest fires consume anything flammable that gets in their way, areas totaling thousands of square miles of forest, brush, and grassland. If left alone, however, they always run out of fuel. The devil virus consumed "human fuel." When its fuel ran out, it simply came to a halt. Yet the virus still exists, though mutated into a far milder form. Influenza pandemics struck in 1957 and 1968, bringing death to 2.5 million people in all. Scientists have proven that the viruses causing those pandemics were descended from their 1918 ancestor.[46]

Many of the people who recovered from the second-wave strain bore its aftereffects for months, even for life. For example, "recovering" poet Robert Frost wondered, "What bones are they that rub together so unpleasantly in the middle of you . . . ? I don't know whether I'm strong enough to write a letter yet." Frost was lucky; eventually he wrote some of his best poems. Still, medical records cite survivors who permanently lost their senses of smell and taste. Some suffered from disorders of the heart, lungs, kidneys, and eyes. Former patients hiccupped for days without letup. Others had hallucinations, seeing menacing spiders, snakes, and bats. "Sleeping sickness" plagued a special group of victims, causing them to sleep and sleep yet awaken exhausted.[47]

Here we may expand Nobel Prize–winning biologist Peter Medawar's definition of a virus: for humanity, the devil virus was the worst piece of bad news that nature *ever* wrapped up in protein. What could science do about it?

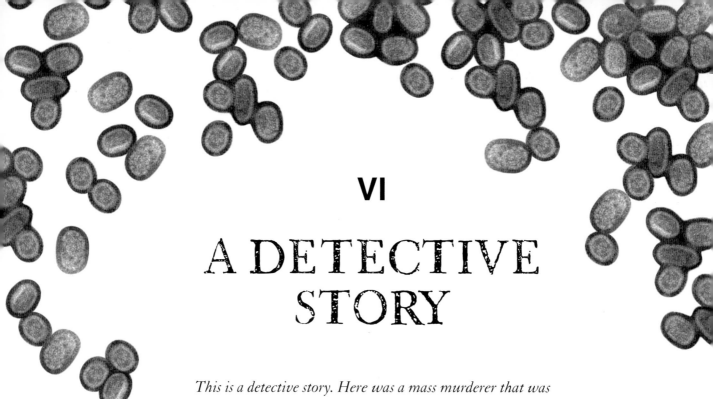

VI

A DETECTIVE STORY

This is a detective story. Here was a mass murderer that was around 80 years ago and who's never been brought to justice. And what we're doing is trying to find the murderer.
—Dr. Jeffery K. Taubenberger, 1998

THE SEARCH BEGINS

With the passing of the third wave, the great pandemic all but vanished from the news. This is not surprising, since forgetfulness is a very human quality, a way of setting aside bad experiences, allowing oneself to go on with living. Historian Alfred W. Crosby confirms this. While glancing at the *Readers' Guide to Periodical Literature* for the period from 1919 to 1921, he made a startling discovery: thirteen inches of column space devoted to references to baseball stories, but only eight inches to stories about influenza. Moreover, few of the leading college history textbooks even mentioned the pandemic, and those that did gave it only a few brief sentences. It was as if humanity were suffering from amnesia, blocking out a painful experience over which it had no control. That is why Crosby titled his classic 1976 book *America's Forgotten Pandemic: The Influenza of 1918.*[1]

Similarly, biographies of leading physicians barely touch on the tragedy. When Victor Vaughan wrote about the war years in his autobiography, *A Doctor's Memories,* he dismissed the flu outright: "I am not going into the history of the influenza epidemic. It encircled the world . . . flaunting its red flag in the face of science." The coauthors of William Welch's biography gave a mere three paragraphs of a 539-page book to this monumental disaster. After ranking it among the "most destructive epidemics of military history," they abruptly changed the subject. For both Vaughan and Welch, as for so many other physicians, the pandemic highlighted the failure of scientific medicine, to which they had devoted their adult lives. It was a stunning letdown after the advances of the previous half century.[2]

For others, however, forgetfulness was not a plan for the future. As one physician observed, the pandemic was "an appalling demonstration of man's hopelessness and ignorance."

But it was also a challenge that science dared not ignore.[3]

There were those who tried to meet the challenge, even as the pandemic raged. Medical researchers set out in various directions. In seeking the cause of influenza, at first most accepted the findings of a German scientist named Richard Pfeiffer. In 1892, Pfeiffer had discovered a bacillus, a rod-shaped bacterium, in the lungs of flu patients. Here, he announced, was the villain. In 1918, doctors doing autopsies found "Pfeiffer's bacillus" in microscope studies of lung tissue from dead soldiers. Believing the bacterium caused influenza, they prepared vaccines to jolt the immune system into action. The vaccines' failure, however, proved that the bacillus did not cause influenza. We now know that the devil virus simply made it easier for normal throat bacteria to infect the lungs.[4]

Meanwhile, Dr. Joseph Goldberger (1874–1929), a U.S. Public Health Service researcher, followed another research path. Goldberger wanted to know how influenza really spread. In pursuing this aim,

Joseph Goldberger, an American physician and epidemiologist employed by the U.S. Public Health Service. (Date unknown)

he experimented on healthy men, a method now illegal in the civilized world.

On November 18, 1918, exactly a week after the armistice, Goldberger visited Deer Island Prison in Boston Harbor. The prisoners were sailors serving time for offenses such as desertion, theft, fighting, and striking a superior. As the doctor looked on, guards lined up a batch of prisoners, surly, tattooed fellows with an attitude. Goldberger explained that he needed fifty men for "certain influenza experiments." The only requirement: they must not have had influenza that year. Prisoners who volunteered, and lived, would get a

pardon, be allowed to return to regular duty at full pay, and have their records wiped clean. "Volunteers," a guard bellowed, "one step forward." Sixty-seven, not fifty, men decided they would be better off with a few days of the flu than years in a navy prison.[5]

A boat took them to nearby Gallops Island, a quarantine station with a large influenza ward. Goldberger then tried everything he could think of to infect his human guinea pigs. He swabbed and sprayed pure Pfeiffer's bacillus into their noses, throats, and eyes. He injected them with blood and a soup of all sorts of bacteria taken from flu patients' noses and throats. For good measure, he exposed each man to two seriously ill patients. The men had to let patients breathe, cough, and sneeze into their faces—they even lay in bed with them for hours. The result? Nobody caught the flu, for reasons still unknown, and, as promised, the men were released. "Perhaps," Goldberger said in conclusion, "if we have learned anything, it is that we are not quite sure what we know about the disease."[6]

Not quite sure! That put it

mildly. Everything about influenza remained mysterious, and perhaps unknowable, in 1918. What caused the infection? Where did it come from? How did it attack? How did it spread? Why did it go away? Could it ever return? Ahead lay decades of painstaking research to make the devil virus reveal its secrets.

BREAKTHROUGHS

Medical researchers, driven by curiosity and their wish to settle scores, moved on several fronts. Even in the midst of the pandemic, they began to document it. Over the years, they amassed a vast array of official reports, detailed studies, articles in medical journals, personal accounts, graphs, and statistical tables. These would provide a factual basis, a jumping-off point, for future research. Even a failed experiment had value, because it ruled out an approach, pointing researchers in other, more promising directions.

The first breakthrough came in February 1933. Scientists Wilson Smith, Christopher H. Andrewes, and Patrick P. Laidlaw of England's National Institute for Medical Research set out to find the cause of the disease in a special way. They washed the throats of flu patients with a sterile liquid, then passed the liquid through filters with such tiny pores that bacteria, if present, could not get through. Finally, they put the filtered liquid into the noses of laboratory mice and guinea pigs, none of which got sick.

The researchers then repeated the experiment with two ferrets, relatives of the weasel with sharp teeth and short tempers. Not only did the ferrets get the flu, so did other ferrets in cages nearby. The team reported it had found "the *primary* infective agent in epidemic influenza," which it called an airborne virus. Three years later, another English scientist, C. H. Stuart-Harris, got the flu after a ferret sneezed in his face. Harris was thrilled because this proved beyond doubt that the virus reached humans through the air. At about the same time, Richard E. Shope, an American researcher, proved that pigs could get the virus, probably from their human handlers. But what *was* a virus—really? And what did a virus look like? Only a better microscope could reveal the answers.[7]

Though microscopes had vastly

improved since the 1600s, the most powerful glass-lens devices enlarged objects only 2,000 times at best. It took a revolution in technology to reveal submicroscopic objects. That happened in the late 1930s, with the electron microscope. A German invention, this device focuses a beam of electrons—charges of electricity arranged around the nucleus of atoms—on an object. It then projects the resulting image onto a screen magnified up to 10 million times. The electron microscope gave birth to the science of virology. Instead of merely *knowing* that flu viruses existed, now researchers could *see* them in every detail, study them, and learn how they worked. But the viruses they saw were merely the current strain, not the devil virus of 1918, which had vanished, burned out during the third wave.

By the early 1940s, virologists had identified the protein spikes that enable the flu virus to stick to a cell's outer wall, penetrate it, and then allow the next viral generation to break out. In 1944, at the height of the Second World War, a team led by Oswald T. Avery Jr. at New York's Rockefeller University Hospital, one of the nation's chief research institutions, proved that certain genes are made of DNA. Later research revealed that flu virus genes consist of RNA.

The year 1944 also saw the first effective flu vaccine. Then as now, drug companies grew active viruses in their laboratories by implanting them in fertilized chicken eggs, an ideal growing medium. Once injected into an egg, a droplet of virus

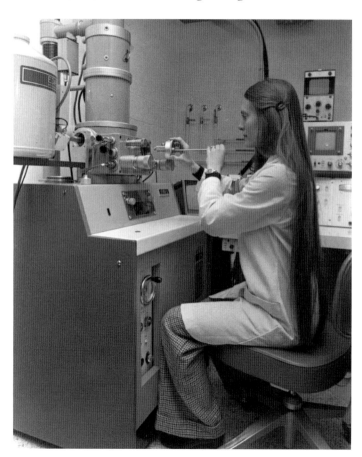

A student using an early scanning electron microscope. (1974)

multiplies until, after a few days, it has become a teaspoonful of new viruses. At that point, technicians remove them, deactivate them chemically, filter out any impurities, and package them for use by health professionals. It takes 150,000 chicken eggs to make a 250-gallon batch of deactivated flu virus. Supplying America with enough vaccine for a normal flu season requires scores of batches and millions of eggs.[8]

It takes between four and six months to manufacture flu vaccines. These, however, are imperfect and cannot always prevent the disease. Nevertheless, the immune system "sees" the invader as foreign, and its memory cells spring into action against a virus related to a previous year's strain. So even if infected, patients have milder symptoms and a shorter recovery time.

However, flu viruses never stop mutating. Because they constantly drift and shift, the current year's vaccine may give little, if any, immunity to the mutations in the next year's virus. As a result, drug companies must constantly change the makeup of their vaccines. Usually, a vaccine is "trivalent," a mixture of what researchers think will be the coming year's three most common viral strains.

Two agencies tell drug companies what strains they must include. Since 1948, experts from the World Health Organization (WHO), an agency of the United Nations, have monitored flu viruses throughout the world. WHO teams track mutations of known strains, looking for signs that they are dangerously close to becoming able to jump from human to human. The other agency, the Centers for Disease Control and Prevention (CDC for short), a branch of the U.S. Department of Health and Human Services, also monitors flu viruses. The agencies' cooperation is an important milestone. Throughout history, people never had warning that a major killer disease was on the way. Now they do. Every February, WHO and CDC virologists hold a "flu meeting" to check their findings and select the strains the drug companies should include in the following year's vaccine. Because it takes six months to make enough vaccine for the seasonal outbreak, companies need to get an early start.

Since 2002, physicians have relied

on two weapons to fight the flu virus *after* it invades lung cells. Sold under the trade names Tamiflu (a pill) and Relenza (an inhalation mist), these drugs act like Krazy Glue. When the protein spikes of next-generation viruses try to tear open an infected lung cell, the drugs clump the viruses together on the cell's inner surface. Immobilized and trapped, the viruses cannot infect nearby cells, and the infection is halted in its tracks. The only drawback is that, for these drugs to work, a person must take them no more than forty-eight hours after symptoms appear. Yet no one knows how long the drugs will continue to be effective. Owing to its constant mutations, the flu virus is likely to find a way to neutralize the drugs,

Tamiflu, the trade name of oseltamivir, an antiviral medication used to treat and prevent influenza.

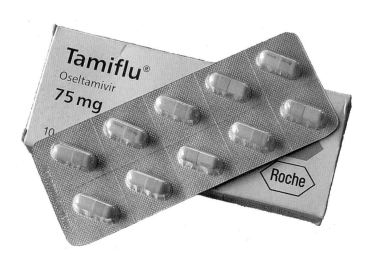

just as bacteria eventually "learn" to resist antibiotics. Change rules nature; nothing stays the same forever. In virology, change also guarantees researchers lifelong employment.

HUNTING THE 1918 KILLER

Given the ever-changing flu virus, scientists are certain another pandemic is inevitable. Pathologist Jeffery K. Taubenberger, whom we will soon get to know better, puts it this way: "The problem is, it happened before. . . . And a lot of people ask me, What's the chance of another pandemic like 1918? The answer is, I have no idea. But if you ask me what the chance of another flu pandemic of *some* kind is, I'll tell you. It's one hundred percent. And I'd like to be ready, wouldn't you?"[9]

Being ready requires knowledge of the long-gone devil virus. What made it unique? What made it so lethal? As mutations create new viral strains today, researchers can look for genetic similarities to those in the 1918 strain. "And if you find a virus that's got them," says Taubenberger, "hey, heads up. This is Bad Virus."

It may be impossible to prevent a

Pathologist Jeffery K. Taubenberger was the first to sequence the genome of the influenza virus that caused the 1918 epidemic. (Date unknown)

Sweden, Hultin enrolled at Iowa State University, which has a first-rate program of study. The following year, he overheard a visiting virologist discuss the 1918 pandemic. So far, the visitor said, nobody had found a trace of the killer virus. The best way to find one, he suggested, was to take lung samples from victims buried in permafrost, ground so frozen that it never thaws, most likely in Alaska. Hultin was fascinated. "I heard that, and my God, then I knew. That was the subject for my PhD. That was *it*," he later told an interviewer.[11]

In 1867, the United States bought Alaska from Russia. A half century later, Alaska was still a wilderness.

pandemic, but it may be possible to prepare to fight one by making a vaccine before it gets going. Yet there is a problem—a very serious one. Flu viruses are extremely fragile; they decay almost immediately after a victim dies. Luckily, finding the virus's remains became the mission of a unique man.[10]

His name is Johan Hultin. In 1949, the twenty-four-year-old took a break from his medical studies to earn a doctorate in microbiology, the science of microscopic organisms. A citizen of

ALASKA

BREVIG MISSION

ANCHORAGE

Gold miners' camps, villages inhabited mostly by white people, and tiny Inuit (sometimes called Eskimo) settlements dotted the countryside. Transportation was chiefly by snowshoe, boat, and dogsled.

On October 20, 1918, the steamship *Victoria,* out of Seattle, Washington, docked at Nome, on the southern tip of Alaska's Seward Peninsula, with tons of supplies and sacks of mail. When *Victoria* sailed, several sailors infected with the devil virus were on board, though they did not yet show symptoms. Within a day or two of the ship's arrival, however, half of the town's 2,000-odd white residents had the flu. Many died. Fear reigned. Ebenezer Evans, a schoolteacher, reported: "As one walked the streets of Nome, it seemed a city of the dead." Travelers soon spread the infection to larger, more distant towns like Anchorage and Fairbanks.[12]

Before getting sick themselves, traders and mail carriers delivered the killer virus to the native population. The Inuit were "virgin soil"—that is, all but defenseless against diseases originating outside their area. Geographic isolation deprives the human immune system of chances to "update" itself, to adapt to novel diseases. Should these diseases manage to reach them, victims lack the memory cells to kick-start an immune reaction. So, finding no opposition, the virus easily slashed through the remote Inuit settlements.

When terrible rumors reached Nome, city officials asked gold miners to inspect the backcountry. Stunned, the miners found the disease had devastated the Inuit community. Despairing people, panicked by horrific symptoms, committed suicide. Unable to hunt moose, seals, and walrus, entire families died of starvation. Huskies, Arctic sled dogs, are little more than domesticated wolves. Though they are loyal and obedient when well fed, hunger makes them ferocious. A report stated:

In many cases were found living children between their dead parents, huddling close to the bodies for warmth; and it was found that [sled dogs] . . . had managed to reach the bodies of the Natives and had eaten them, only a mass of bones and blood evidence of their having been people.

Gold miners had to build fires to soften the permafrost so they could dig graves to bury victims' remains.[13]

Now, after thirty-three years, Johan Hultin planned to search for the virus in those remains. He'd already visited Alaska during his 1949 summer vacation with Otto Geist, a fellow scientist, looking for bones of prehistoric horses. Hultin wrote Geist, who referred him to Christian missionaries. They helped him get church records from isolated Alaskan villages, giving the names of those who had died during the pandemic and the location of their graves. When Hultin checked this data against a permafrost map, he decided the best place to look was Brevig Mission, a tiny Inuit village a hundred miles north of Nome. The village had been home to eighty people in 1918; flu killed seventy-two of them within five days, November 15–20.

Pathologist Johan Hultin at the Alaskan dig site where victims of the 1918 flu were buried in a mass grave. (1997)

Missionaries melted a patch of permafrost, buried the dead in a mass grave, and marked the site with two wooden crosses.

In June 1951, Hultin traveled alone to Brevig Mission, his expenses paid by a small grant from Iowa State. After he explained his purpose, village elders gave him permission to open the grave and take samples of lung tissue from the bodies. Public health workers had vaccinated villagers against smallpox, so the elders understood why Hultin's findings might help prevent another flu pandemic.

Working by himself, Hultin thawed the grave site with fires and put in sixteen to eighteen hours a day, digging. The work was hard and sweaty, but he kept going with

pick and shovel. At a depth of six feet, he found the body of a little girl. "She was a child about six years old," he recalled. "She was beautiful, with her black braids. She was well preserved, and I knew there'd be many, many more." Hultin called for help, and three scientists came from Iowa State. The team enlarged the hole, removing bits of lung from five other bodies. To prevent decay, Hultin sealed these samples in thermos bottles with dry ice taken from fire extinguishers.[14]

Back at Iowa State, Hultin thawed the samples and sprayed tiny amounts of the dissolved lung tissue into ferrets' noses. Yet, try as he might, his experiments failed; none of the animals came down with influenza. "Oh," Hultin recalled years later, "it was disappointing, disappointing. I used up all the material, and got nothing from it." Though Hultin never finished his doctorate, he graduated from medical school and spent nearly his entire career as a pathologist at a hospital in California. Yet he did not take defeat easily. Hultin's failure, like a dull toothache, continued to nag at him. If another chance ever came, he said, he'd

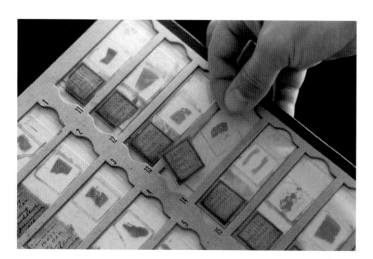

Preserved lung specimen slides from the U.S. 1918 flu epidemic.

gladly take up the hunt for the devil virus. Dr. Jeffery K. Taubenberger gave him that chance.[15]

Born in 1961, Taubenberger grew up in a German immigrant family; his father was a career officer in the U.S. army. Jeffery became interested in science at an early age. What fascinated him was that scientists were, in a sense, overgrown children. "Scientists," he says, "are people who refuse to grow up. You know that kids are incredibly curious; the first thing they do when they start talking is to ask Why? Why, why, why? Because they want to know. . . . [But] when children ask why-why-why, they expect someone else to give them the answer. When scientists ask why-why-why . . . they want to find the answer themselves."[16]

After graduating from medical school, Taubenberger became a civilian pathologist at the Armed Forces Institute of Pathology (AFIP). The AFIP was a gift of President Abraham Lincoln, the "Great Emancipator," who dealt the deathblow to slavery during the Civil War. In 1862, a year before issuing the Emancipation Proclamation, Lincoln created the AFIP by executive order. Its aim

was to collect examples of all aspects of human disease. Though the AFIP shut its doors in 2011 because of congressionally ordered base closures, many of its activities were taken over by a new organization, the Joint Pathology Center (JPC) in Bethesda, Maryland.

Today, the JPC "library" has over three million items. Technicians fix each item in formalin, a chemical preservative, and then embed it in a half-inch-thick wax wafer about the size of a thumbnail. To study a specimen, scientists use a machine to slice the wafer thinner than the thinnest paper and then dye the tissue a color that highlights its features. Finally, they mount it on a glass slide to look at with whatever type of microscope they think can best reveal its secrets.

Taubenberger is an expert in restoring genetic material found in decayed tissue samples, a difficult, time-consuming task requiring specialized equipment and methods and infinite patience. It is like putting each tiny splinter of a shattered glass windowpane in its right place. In 1995, the scientist wondered if he could find the 1918 flu virus in lung tissue from autopsies of soldiers who'd died during the pandemic. "I really wanted to see if there was some way we could make use of this vast, wonderful collection," he recalled.[17]

Taubenberger ordered seventy-eight samples from the AFIP collection. He and colleague Ann H. Reid soon found "really really teeny tiny" fragments of flu virus genes in lung tissue from Roscoe Vaughan, a twenty-one-year-old private who died at Fort Jackson, South Carolina, in September 1918. Though able to "sequence" these fragments—assemble them in the correct order—they had too few to draw a detailed picture of the elusive genes. The researchers had hit a brick wall. To update the scientific record, Taubenberger published their findings in the March 1997 issue of the magazine *Science*. That article caught the eye of Johan Hultin.[18]

August 1997 found Hultin retired and living in San Francisco. Though a few weeks short of his seventy-third birthday, he was dynamic, bursting with energy. As he liked to say, "I'm going to settle down when I get old." Physical activity—skiing, hiking, camping, mountain climbing—kept him in top shape.[19]

Upon reading Taubenberger's article, Hultin wrote him about his Alaskan trip and failed experiments. "If you need more specimens, let me know, and I will go back to Alaska. I've been there before. I know where it is. I can go back," he said. A few days later, Taubenberger called, asking, "When can you go?" Hultin replied, "Next week."[20]

After forty-six years, Hultin returned to Brevig Mission alone, traveling at his own expense, $3,200 withdrawn from his bank account. Again he explained his aim to the village council, and again he was allowed to explore the mass grave. "Would you like some help?" a council member asked. Hultin did, and four young Inuit men were assigned to work beside him.[21]

On the third day of digging, at a depth of seven feet, they found four frozen bodies, including that of an obese woman in her thirties. She was particularly well preserved. "Her lungs were magnificent, full of blood," Hultin recalled. "I sat on an upside-down pail and looked at this [body], and I got the flash in my mind. Maybe this is where I can find it." So he named her Lucy, from *lux,*

An Inuit woman and child. Frozen bodies of flu-stricken Inuit were instrumental in Hultin's quest for information about the influenza virus. (1906)

Taubenberger and Hultin, known as the "Indiana Jones of the scientific set." (Date unknown)

the Latin word for "light," hoping she would shed a bright light on her killer.[22]

Hultin removed Lucy's lungs and parts of the others' lungs with gardening shears he'd borrowed from his wife. After he and his Inuit helpers closed the grave, Hultin sliced up and placed the specimens in preserving fluid, then wrapped, labeled, and packed them up in four identical batches. Back in San Francisco, he sent the packages—by different carriers, to ensure at least one made it—to Taubenberger, who called

ten days later. "Johan," he said, "we have it. . . . We have lots of specimen, great material, and this is going to be wonderful."[23]

Taubenberger's team soon found what they were looking for. "It was absolutely thrilling! Absolutely amazingly thrilling!" he told an interviewer. There, projected onto the screen of an electron microscope, were images of bits of influenza genes nearly identical to those in the sample from Private Vaughan. From that moment on, "flu just took over my life," the scientist recalled. Yet it was not until October 2005 that his team assembled all eight viral genes in their correct order. Even so, no one could explain exactly why the devil virus behaved the way it had. Nevertheless, at last scientists knew what mutations were most likely to trigger another 1918-like pandemic.[24]

H5N1: AN EMERGING MENACE

On May 21, 1997, three months before Johan Hultin left for Alaska, a three-year-old boy named Lam Hoi-ka played with a cuddly yellow chick at a Hong Kong day-care center. Six days later, he died of an infection that caused his lungs, brain, liver, and kidneys to fail. To find the exact cause of death, city health officials sent freeze-dried samples of infected tissue to laboratories in Europe and America. The samples revealed that the child was the first person ever to die of "bird flu." Virologists classify the strain that killed him as H5N1, based on the protein spikes it uses to break into and out of cells.

CDC investigators rushed to Hong Kong. After careful analysis, they found no further evidence that H5N1 had crossed over to humans. "It had not spread to even one other person, so we just wrote it off as a freak occurrence . . . and that would be the end of it," said a relieved Keiji Fukuda, the team leader. He'd spoken too soon. By December, eighteen more people had come down with bird flu; six of them died.[25]

The Hong Kong victims except Lam Hoi-ka had something in common: all had recently visited or worked in markets that sold live chickens, ducks, and geese. Flu viruses, we recall, swap genes from birds, humans, and pigs inside a pig "mixing vessel." Swapping may allow a new viral strain to jump to people, which is bad enough, but if people can transmit the infection to one another, it is disastrous. Before 1997, virologists believed a bird flu virus could not bypass the pig mixing vessel and infect humans directly. Yet, for reasons still not fully understood, H5N1 did exactly that in 1997.

A total stranger to the human immune system, H5N1 kills most of its victims. In the sixteen years after the Hong Kong outbreak, it infected more than 600 people, killing nearly 400, an astonishing 60 percent of victims. (The 1918 devil virus infected much of the human race yet killed

Strains of the bird flu continued to reoccur in Hong Kong. Here, officials wearing masks and protective suits dispose of chickens following the discovery of the virus in a wholesale market. (2014)

only 2.5 percent of its victims.) The only good thing is that, while H5N1 may jump from birds to humans, it stops there—at least for the present. But virologists fear it is only a matter of time before it mutates to the point where it can travel from person to person, igniting a pandemic.[26]

This is why WHO and CDC virus hunters focus on China. It is the world's largest nation in population, with about a fifth of the human race, and the third largest in area; only Russia and Canada have more territory. China also has the world's largest number of domesticated birds.

Hong Kong is the most densely packed city on the planet. Guangdong Province, in which it lies, has 86 million people, tens of millions of pigs, and about 650,000 birds per square mile.[27]

Rice, Guangdong's chief food crop, grows in water. Farmers raise ducks on their farms, but also on flooded rice paddies. Wild waterfowl share these paddies. Although they have H5N1 in their guts, it seems not to bother them. However, wild birds defecate in paddy water; scientists have found an estimated ten billion flu viruses in a single quart.

As a result, it is impossible to prevent wild birds from infecting their domesticated cousins. As Hong Kong virologist Yi Guan explains, "I cannot control them. I cannot lock my sky."[28]

Chinese farmers from all over the country send their ducks and geese to urban poultry markets. Before being sold, these birds are kept in crowded cages along with chickens, a favorite food throughout Asia. "Without chicken, there will not be a banquet," says a Chinese proverb. Since customers demand freshness, most chickens are sold in "wet markets"— wet because butchers kill the birds right in front of their customers. Hygiene is not a high priority in these places. Buyers and sellers are invariably exposed to bird blood, feathers, and droppings, and therefore to H5N1. Virus-laden droppings also contaminate feed, vehicles, shoes, clothing, and water.[29]

A gram (0.035 ounce) of H5N1-containing duck feces can infect more than a million birds. The effects are as horrific for chickens as the 1918 devil virus was for people. H5N1 simply "melts" chickens. "The invader commandeers every organ and tissue of a bird, from the top of its comb to the tips of its . . . feet. The [chickens] bleed from their eyes, beaks, and anuses. One moment they are pecking away; the next they fall over dead. In the end they just 'melt out,' resembling rubber caricatures of themselves."[30]

Well aware of the danger, investigators continually inspect Chinese poultry markets. The slightest trace of H5N1 brings death not only to infected birds but to every other bird as well. In December 1997, after several people died of bird flu, Hong Kong authorities decided to stop the feared epidemic before it began. Over a weekend, health workers killed every chicken, duck, and goose in the city, over 1.5 million birds in all. "Everyone is covered with protective gear—moon suits and all," a virologist wrote. "They put the birds in bags and then used gas on them. Then they were deposited in the landfills."[31]

The Hong Kong slaughter was only a temporary fix; it could not eliminate bird flu. Radiating from China, H5N1 has reached South Korea, North Korea, Japan, Vietnam, Cambodia, Laos, Thailand,

India, Pakistan, Indonesia, and the Philippines. In those countries, more than 400 million chickens and other domesticated birds were killed between 2004 and 2010, at an estimated cost of $20 billion. Scarcity caused prices to rise, affecting the poor, those least able to afford this protein-rich food.[32]

Migrating waterfowl have spread H5N1 as far away as Europe and the United States. In 2003, the Dutch military slaughtered 30 million chickens. Police officers also raided private homes, searching for pet chickens to kill. In 2004, H5N1 roared through Asia again. In Vietnam, health workers burned chickens alive, not to be cruel but to make sure they destroyed the virus as quickly as possible. In Thailand, virologists ordered 11 million birds killed; they also learned that the fiercest animals were no match for this tiny virus. Bangkok, the capital, is home to the world-famous Sriracha Tiger Zoo. When H5N1 killed 45 tigers, zookeepers removed raw chicken, bought at a local market, from the tigers' diet. No matter; infected tigers passed the disease to other tigers, forcing keepers to destroy another 102 animals. Before 2004, tigers were thought to be immune to bird flu. Obviously, H5N1 was mutating, with scary results.[33]

As the bird flu spread, millions of fowl were exterminated and dumped in quarantined locations. (2016)

In 2015, bird flu reached the United States in a big way. Apparently, migrating Canada geese brought H5N1 to the Midwest, a major producer of chickens and turkeys. The disease spread so rapidly that public health officials ordered 46 million birds destroyed. Most were in Iowa, the nation's top egg-producing state, and Minnesota, the leader in turkey production. As a result, the price of eggs and products made from eggs skyrocketed. Thanksgiving turkeys, too, became more expensive.[34]

Americans today are well aware of the threat posed by pandemics. Novelists and filmmakers have created fictional accounts of viral catastrophes. Michael Crichton's *The Andromeda Strain,* Stephen King's *The Stand,* and Richard Matheson's *I Am Legend* deal with the aftermath of mysterious viruses attacking a virgin population. Scott Z. Burns's film *Contagion* deals with a pandemic originating in Hong Kong when bats drop virus-laden feces into a pigpen. The bat and pig viruses mutate, and the resulting virus destroys the social order, killing twenty-six million people worldwide until a vaccine finally halts its spread. (So far, scientists have not reported *any* recombinations of bat and pig viruses.)[35]

Some fictional accounts deal just with flu pandemics. In the *Twilight* book series by Stephenie Meyer, which was also made into movies, the parents of one character die of "Spanish flu" in 1918; he is saved by being turned into a vampire. The Internet, too, has heightened awareness of influenza. A 2017 search of Google yielded 280,000 hits for the phrase "Spanish flu epidemic" and 1.7 million for "flu epidemic history." Since 2000, there have been at least twenty-three novels dealing with the theme of flu pandemics.

Fictional scenarios, shocking as they may be, pale in comparison with what we could expect from a full-blown H5N1 pandemic. "The world just has no idea what it's going to see if this thing happens," says Scott Dowell, a virologist working in Thailand. "We are past ifs. Whether it's tomorrow or next year or some other time, nobody knows for sure. The clock is ticking. We just don't know what time it is." Virologist Robert Webster agrees. Humanity is sleeping on a time bomb, he told an interviewer, "and there will be no place for any of us to hide. Not in the United States or in Europe or in a bunker somewhere."[36]

Should H5N1 bird flu adapt to humans, it would engulf the planet not in weeks or months, as the devil virus did, but almost overnight. Our world in the twenty-first century is in an era of globalization, more closely connected than ever before. Every day, many thousands of travelers cross oceans and continents aboard jet airliners. As a result, humankind is ready-made for crowd diseases, particularly influenza. A single infected passenger could pass H5N1 to everyone aboard a plane. Upon landing, those travelers would infect others, and so on, until the disease raged everywhere. According to a 2009 U.S. Defense Department study, H5N1 would sicken about 90 million Americans and cause about 2 million deaths.[37]

The pandemic would have a cascading effect. Always eager for a sensational story, the media, particularly television, would spread panic. The labor force, because of sick-

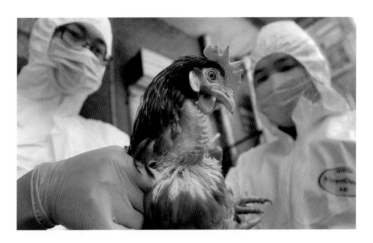

Researchers examine a rooster. (2015)

ness, fear, or having to tend to sick family members, would not report for work. Soon the economy would come to a standstill as industries shut down, businesses closed, and unemployment soared. Growing shortages of vital goods, from food to fuel to medical supplies, would bring chaos. Government would cease to function. Hospitals, mortuaries, and cemeteries would overflow as in 1918, only more so. Taken by surprise, drug companies would not have the time, or the healthy scientific personnel, to develop a new generation of vaccines. A vaccine against H5N1 would not become available for months after work got under way. By the time the pandemic burned out, civilization as we know it would have collapsed, leaving in its wake famines and wars claiming millions of additional lives.[38]

This is a grim picture, but there is more. Without intending to, scientists may have already brought the catastrophe closer.

ENGINEERING DOOMSDAY

Dr. Ron Fouchier is a virologist at the Erasmus Medical Center in Rotterdam, Netherlands. Like Jeffery Taubenberger, he became fascinated with influenza early in his career. Fouchier knows that viruses do not depend on scientists to gain new mutations; they mutate all the time in nature. So he decided to focus his research on whether H5N1 might mutate into a form that easily spreads among humans and what that form might be. This was dangerous work, and he had to take special precautions to keep his virus samples from escaping. Fouchier's superiors agreed and built a 1,000-square-foot laboratory just for him. It is really a fortress, where everyone works in space suits in sealed compartments with filtered air to protect them from infection.

Fouchier tried to transfer bird flu from one ferret to another. To do this, he explained, he "mutated the hell out of H5N1"; that is, by using various advanced technologies, he changed the order of two of the segments in the virus's eight genes. When he injected the genes into ferrets, nothing happened; the animals were as frisky and ornery as ever. Then, Fouchier said, "someone finally convinced me to do something really, really stupid." On a hot July day in 2011, he squirted mutated H5N1 virus into the nose of one ferret. Success! And when that ferret got sick, he put infected mucus from it into the nose of a second ferret. After repeating this ten times, airborne droplets of H5N1 infected healthy ferrets in cages next to the sick ones, and three out of four of them died. Fouchier had "taught"

Ferrets are sometimes used by scientists to study influenza in humans. (Date unknown)

H5N1 to spread from ferret to ferret on its own.[39]

In September 2011, Fouchier attended the annual meeting of the European Scientific Working Group on Influenza. "This virus is airborne and as efficiently transmitted as the seasonal [flu] virus," he announced, adding, "This is very bad news." The astonished scientists sat in silence, hardly believing their ears. What Fouchier had done was truly bad news—the stuff of horror fiction. Ferrets catch the flu in the same way as humans; that is why virologists prefer them for experiments. Now Fouchier had used this knowledge to make H5N1 contagious, without its having to combine with other viruses in a pig mixing vessel.[40]

Fouchier's announcement set off a storm in the international flu research community. One group of virologists defended his experiments. Yes, he had made H5N1 contagious in the laboratory, they argued, but nature could do the same, given enough time. By discovering what genes had to change to make this happen, Fouchier had created an early-warning system, they said. Now scientists could look out for

such changes and, if they found any, rush development of vaccines before a pandemic got under way.[41]

Critics praised Fouchier's zeal for protecting the public's health. But they thought him reckless, too. His mutated virus was too unstable, too stealthy, to keep in check, they declared. "This research should never have been done," growled Dr. Richard H. Ebright, a weapons expert at Rutgers University in New Jersey. Mutated H5N1 would "inevitably escape, and within a decade." When this happened, warned Dr. Donald A. Henderson of the University of Pittsburgh, H5N1 "would be the ultimate organism as far as destruction of population is concerned." But these critics had spoken too soon; Fouchier had not created the ultimate killing agent. Another research team did that.[42]

Dr. Yoshihiro Kawaoka, a virologist at the University of Wisconsin's Institute for Influenza Viral Research, wanted to improve flu vaccines. To do this, Kawaoka decided he first needed special viruses to test the vaccines on. So he took H1N1 genes from a strain related to the 1918 devil virus, then

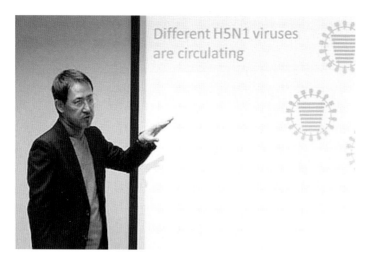

Different H5N1 viruses
are circulating

Virologist Yoshihiro
Kawaoka, who,
in the interest of
scientific discovery,
created a new
variation of the flu
virus that has no
known vaccine.
(2013)

blended them with H5N1 genes, creating an entirely new virus. For good measure, Kawaoka mutated the new virus four times, until he got what he called "a real humdinger of a virus."[43]

That was an understatement. When Kawaoka announced the results of his experiments in 2011, fellow scientists and the media pounced. What he had created was a supervirus, a thing not found in nature. His virus not only can spread quickly through the air but is deadlier than any known virus, because it evades the human immune system. Should it ever escape from his laboratory, it would find humanity defenseless. No wonder critics called Kawaoka's work "absolutely crazy." "It's madness, folly," said virologist Simon

Wain-Hobson of the Pasteur Institute in Paris, a major research center. "What the F are you doing?"[44]

The publication of researchers' findings in scientific journals is crucial to the search for truth. Publication makes ideas and experiments available to scientists the world over. It allows them to keep up with developments in their field, repeat experiments, verify or refute others' findings, and discover additional things about a subject. Freedom of the press, too, is a core principle of democracy, because the public must get the information it needs to check abuses by government officials. As a practical matter, though, we must strike a balance between the right to know and the right to live. No one, for example, questions the federal government's right to keep secrets relating to national defense. Similarly, sharing scientific findings can endanger countless lives.

As for H5N1 bird flu, many scientists wanted to keep Fouchier's and Kawaoka's methods and findings secret. "It's just a bad idea for scientists to turn a lethal virus into a lethal and highly contagious virus," said Dr. Thomas Inglesby, director of the Center for Health Security of Pittsburgh Medical Center. "And it's a second bad idea for them to publish just how they did it so others can copy it." On January 11, 2012, the journal *New Scientists* carried an alarming headline: "One Mistake Away from a Worldwide Flu Pandemic." Dr. Michael T. Osterholm, an infectious disease expert, took the matter personally. "Those researchers have all of our lives at the end of their fingers," he said. What if their work got into the wrong hands? Fanatics could use the virus for bioterrorism, terrorism involving the use of toxic biological agents.[45]

The U.S. government had a say in the publication debate because tax dollars helped fund Fouchier's research and Kawaoka's institute. In December 2011, the National Science Advisory Board for Biosecurity, an independent government advisory group, took up the question. At first, it recommended censoring the virologists' reports, omitting key information, before publication. However, the board reversed itself the following year, because, members felt, the benefit of alerting the scientific community to the research outweighed the risk of someone putting it to evil use. The journals

Wearing surgical masks and gowns, technicians make small openings in eggs to prepare vaccines.

Science and *Nature* duly printed articles with full details of the experiments. It remains to be seen how dangerous this information is. We know that anyone with the skill and will, money and equipment, can create a mutated H5N1 supervirus. In October 2014, the White House had second thoughts. It announced that the federal government would stop funding studies aimed at increasing the deadliness and transmission of influenza viruses, at least for the time being. The decision, however, may have come too late.[46]

We live in an age of globalism and terrorism. Globalism brings people together, while terrorism uses violence to create widespread fear to advance a political, social, or religious cause. Terrorists kidnap innocents, explode bombs in crowded places, and hijack airplanes. On September 11, 2001, hijackers crashed two airliners into the twin towers of the World Trade Center in New York City and another plane into the Pentagon, the nation's military nerve center, in Arlington, Virginia. A fourth plane, on its way to the Pentagon, the U.S. Capitol, or the White House, crashed in a field in rural Pennsylvania.

The nineteen 9/11 hijackers were members of al-Qaeda, a radical Muslim group led by a Saudi extremist named Osama bin Laden (later killed by Army Special Forces). Unlike the vast majority of Muslims, those inspired by bin Laden think it a religious duty, commanded by God, to exterminate "infidels." In their eyes, unbelievers are entirely evil—"the scum of the human race," "the rats of the world," "brothers of apes and pigs," the "Party of Satan." Thus, bin Laden said, "we do not have to differentiate between military or civilian. As far as we are concerned, they are all targets." In an essay titled "Under the Shade of the Lances," Sulaiman Abu Ghaith, al-Qaeda's official spokesman, declared: "We have the right to kill four million Americans—two million of them children—and to exile twice as many and wound and cripple hundreds of thousands." Furthermore, terrorists preach that "Muslims who don't hate America sin." These are not mere words, spoken for effect; those who use them mean what they say. Who else today crucifies Christians, beheads them, and drowns them? Who else burns Muslims who disagree with them alive in iron cages? Who else promises to kill every Jew in Israel?[47]

According to terrorist logic, any weapon is legitimate if used in "God's cause." A book by a bin Laden follower, titled *A Treatise on the Ruling Regarding the Use of Weapons of Mass Destruction Against Infidels,* sets no limits upon the use of weapons of mass destruction. Since the 1980s, terrorist groups have tried to get hold of nuclear, chemical, and biological weapons. "Nuclear War," they insist, "is the Solution for the Destruction of the United States." Biological weapons, however, could do the job more thoroughly.[48]

On December 7, 2011, Secretary of State Hillary Clinton marked the seventieth anniversary of Japan's attack on Pearl Harbor with a speech. During the Biological Weapons Convention in Geneva, Switzerland, she cautioned against the threat of bioterrorism. "There are warning signs," she said, "[that al-Qaeda] made a call to arms for—and I

A New York police officer stands near a wanted poster in the financial district of New York City one week after the terrorist attacks of 9/11. Printed on a full page of a New York newspaper, the poster features Saudi-born militant Osama bin Laden. (September 18, 2001)

quote—brothers with degrees in microbiology or chemistry to develop a weapon of mass destruction." She especially noted that Western laboratories were "making genetic material widely available. This obviously has many benefits for research, but it could potentially be used to assemble the components of a deadly organism."[49]

For "deadly organism," read

"H5N1 bird flu." Unscrupulous scientists might sell samples of the virus to terrorists, just as Abdul Qadeer Khan, Pakistan's leading physicist, sold nuclear-weapon plans to North Korea, Libya, and Iran. Easier yet, anyone can download Ron Fouchier's article from a certain website for $31.50. Extremists are also skilled in using the Internet and social media to circulate instruction manuals with titles like *Biological Weapons.* If we may use an Internet term, such writings have "gone viral."[50]

Mutated H5N1 may be the ultimate terrorist weapon, cheaper to make and easier to use than atomic bombs. Those weapons, awful as they are, require large missiles and airplanes to deliver them to their targets. Bird flu is far more lethal. Terrorist leaders already inspire suicide bombers to kill as many "unbelievers" as possible. In doing so, "human bombs" seek "martyrdom," touted as a sure ticket to paradise. Similarly, a fanatic might seek martyrdom by voluntarily becoming infected with mutated H5N1, then boarding a jumbo jet. This would be the worst place to be in the presence of any flu virus. In 1977, for example, when a crowded airliner lost its ventilation system for several hours, an "ordinary" flu virus spread through the cabin with stunning speed; nearly everyone became infected from one sneezing passenger.[51]

Imagine what would happen if a bird-flu "martyr" boarded a jumbo jet today. The disease could spread to everyone aboard, then to everyone those travelers met, and so on, until the pandemic rolled across the globe, killing up to half the human race. The dead would also include innocent Muslims, and even terrorists and their loved ones. Yet to the fanatic, any price is worth paying to rid the world of infidels and assure victory to "God's cause."

A FINAL REFLECTION

Life is neither all good nor all bad. Everyone suffers misfortunes but also has bright moments, however brief they may be. Similarly, we may say that we are worse off today than in 1918, but we are also better off. Scientists' tinkering has made influenza viruses more lethal and capable of spreading from person to person. On the other hand, knowledge of influenza, of what causes it and how it acts, has made us better able to treat it, predict pandemics, and develop vaccines to avoid their worst effects.

The chief lesson we can take from this terrifying disease is the need for humility in the face of nature. Historians Dorothy Pettit and Janice Bailie say it best: "We must treat this microscopic 'mass murderer' with the utmost respect and never doubt its exceptional ability to adapt."[52]

Influenza is what it is. The strains of viruses that cause the disease *will* keep adapting, keep changing—usually as seasonal annoyances, though still lethal for some victims. Scientists will continue to study flu viruses, while organizations like the World Health Organization and the Centers for Disease Control and Prevention will search for genetic changes pointing to the likelihood of a pandemic. When the next pandemic comes, as it surely will someday, perhaps we will be ready to meet it. If we are not, the outcome will be very, very, very dreadful.

NOTES

PROLOGUE: THE GREAT-GRANDDADDY OF THEM ALL

1. John M. Barry, *The Great Influenza: The Epic Story of the Deadliest Plague in History* (New York: Viking Penguin, 2004), 96.

2. Carol R. Byerly, "The U.S. Military and the Influenza Pandemic of 1918–1919," *Public Health Reports,* vol. 125, Supplement 3 (2010): "Influenza Pandemic in the United States," 82–91, www.ncbi.nih.gov/pmc/articles/PMC2862337.

3. Nancy K. Britsow, " 'It's as Bad as Anything Can Be': Patients, Identity, and the Influenza Pandemic," *Public Health Reports,* vol. 125, Supplement 3 (2010): "Influenza Pandemic in the United States," 136, www.ncbi.nih.gov/pmc/articles/PMC2862342.

4. Dorothy A. Pettit and Janice Bailie, *A Cruel Wind: Pandemic Flu in America, 1918–1920* (Murfreesboro, TN: Timberlane Books, 2008), 1. Italics added.

5. Paul W. Ewald, *Evolution of Infectious Disease* (New York: Oxford University Press, 1994), 36.

6. M. Webster Brown, "Historical Medicine: Early Epidemics of Influenza in America," *Medical Journal and Record,* 1932, 449–451; Michael Greger, *Bird Flu: A Virus of Our Own Hatching,* www.birdflubook.org/a.php?id=2; C. W. Potter, "A History of Influenza," *Journal of Applied Microbiology,* 91, no. 4 (October 2001), 575.

7. Niall Johnson and Juergen Muller, "Updating the Accounts: Global Mortality of the 1918–1920 'Spanish' Influenza Pandemic," *Bulletin of the History of Medicine,* 76 (2002), 105–115; Michael T. Osterholm, "Preparing for the Next Pandemic," *Foreign Affairs,* July–August 2005, 26; Gina Bari Kolata, *Flu: The Story of the Great Influenza Epidemic of 1918 and the Search for the Virus That Caused It* (New York: Farrar, Straus and Giroux, 1999), 7.

8. Carol R. Byerly, *Fever of War: The Influenza Epidemic in the U.S. Army During World War I* (New York: New York University Press, 2005), 71–72.

9. Joseph E. Persico, *Eleventh Month, Eleventh Day, Eleventh Hour: Armistice Day, 1918—World War I and Its Violent Climax* (New York: Random House, 2004), 379; Neil Hanson, *Unknown Soldiers: The Story of the Missing of the First World War* (New York: Vintage Books, 2007),

224–225; UNAIDS, "Fact Sheet," www.unaids.org/en/resources/campaigns/2014/2014gap report/factsheet.

10. "U.S. Life Expectancy, 1900–2000," www.mikalac.com/tech/sta/long.htm#1910; Alfred W. Crosby, *America's Forgotten Pandemic: The Influenza of 1918* (1976; repr., New York: Cambridge University Press, 1989), 207; Kolata, *Flu,* 7; Byerly, *Fever of War,* 89; David Thompson, "The Influenza Pandemic's Impact on the U.S. Military in World War I," *Roads to the Great War* (blog), August 29, 2013, roadstothegreatwar-ww1-blogspot-com/2013/08/the -influenza-pandemics-impact-on-us.html.

I: THE PITILESS WAR

1. Arno Karlen, *Man and Microbes: Disease and Plagues in History and Modern Times* (New York: Simon & Schuster, 1996), 21–23.

2. Jared Diamond, *Guns, Germs, and Steel: The Fates of Human Societies* (New York: Norton, 1999), 95, 97; Jared Diamond, "The Worst Mistake in the History of the Human Race," *Discover,* May 1987.

3. Karlen, *Man and Microbes,* 41.

4. Ibid., 39, 52, 57.

5. Exodus 9:14, 9:9.

6. "Thucydides on the Plague," Livius, www.livius.org/pb-pem/peloponnesian_war/war_ t05 .html.

7. Linda Gigante, "Death and Disease in Ancient Rome," www.innominatesociety.com/Articles /Death%20and%20Disease%20in%20Ancient%20Rome.htm; Alison Morton, "The Antonine Plague—the Germs That Killed an Empire," Alison Morton (personal website), alison -morton.com/2011/11/10/the-antonine-plague-the-germs-that-killed-an-empire.

8. Alexandre Yersin (1863–1943), a French physician, discovered the bacterium that causes bubonic plague in 1894. In 1908, researchers proved that rat fleas spread the disease.

9. Procopius, *History of the Wars,* Internet Medieval Sourcebook, "Procopius: The Plague, 542," Fordham University, legacy.fordham.edu/halsall/source/542procopius-plague.asp.

10. John Kelly, *The Great Mortality: An Intimate History of the Black Death, the Most Devastating Plague of All Time* (New York: HarperCollins, 2005), 17.

11. Norman F. Cantor, *In the Wake of the Plague: The Black Death and the World It Made* (New York: Free Press, 2001), 6.

12. Kelly, *The Great Mortality,* 27; Agnolo di Tura, "The Plague in Siena: An Italian Chronicle," in Perry M. Rogers, *Aspects of Western Civilization* (New York: Prentice Hall, 2000), 353–365, posted at Plague Readings, www.u.arizona.edu/~afutrell/w%20civ%2002/plaguereadings .html.

13. Watson Nicholson, *The Historical Sources of Defoe's "Journal of the Plague Year," Illustrated by Extracts from the Original Documents* (1919; repr., Port Washington, NY: Kennikat Press, 1966).

14. Daniel Defoe, *A Journal of the Plague Year* (1722; repr., Thorndike, ME: G. K. Hall, 2000), 30, 78, 98, 123. There are many editions of this classic English work.

15. Ibid., 49, 52, 53, 118–119.

16. Greg Botelho, "Child Who Visited Yosemite National Park Comes Down with the Plague," CNN, August 7, 2015, www.cnn.com/2015/8/06/health/yosemite-plague-child; "Bubonic Plague Diagnosed in Teton County, Yellowstone Visitor," Wyoming Department of Health, www.health.wyo.gov/news/aspx?NewsID=212.

17. "Anthony van Leeuwenhoek," University of California Museum of Paleontology, www.ucmp .berkeley.edu/history/leeuwenhoek.html.

18. Fred R. van Hartesveldt, "The Doctors and the 'Flu': The British Medical Profession's Response to the Influenza Pandemic of 1918–19," *International Social Sciences Review,* 85, nos. 1–2 (Spring–Summer 2010), 29.

19. For Jenner's own writings, see Edward Jenner, *Vaccination Against Smallpox* (Amherst, NY: Prometheus Books, 1996). See also Albert Marrin, *Dr. Jenner and the Speckled Monster: The Search for the Smallpox Vaccine* (New York: Dutton Children's Books, 2002).

20. Roy Porter, *The Greatest Benefit to Mankind: A Medical History of Humanity* (New York: Norton, 1997), 365. This is the best general history of medicine from ancient times to the present day.

21. Ibid., 367.

22. William W. Keen, "Military Surgery in 1861 and 1918," *Annals of the American Academy of Political and Social Science,* 80 (November 1918), 14, 15.

23. Nancy Tomes, "The Making of a Germ Panic, Then and Now," *American Journal of Public Health,* 90, no. 2 (February 2002), 192–194.

24. Andrew D. White, "Theological Opposition to Inoculation, Vaccination, and the Use of Anaesthetics," in *A History of the Warfare of Science with Theology in Christendom* (New York: D. Appleton, 1896), Bob Kobres (personal website), abob.libs.uga.edu/bobk/whitem10.html. See also "Utopian Surgery: Early Arguments Against Anesthesia in Surgery, Dentistry and Childbirth," Hedonistic Imperative, hedweb.com.anesthesia/index.html.

25. Clyde F. Barker, "Thomas Eakins and His Medical Clinics," *Proceedings of the American Philosophical Society,* 153, no. 1 (March 2009), 9, 20.

26. Ibid., 16, 23.

27. Kolata, *Flu,* 258.

28. Sandra M. Tomkins, "The Failure of Expertise: Public Health Policy in Britain During the 1918–19 Influenza Epidemic," *Social History of Medicine,* 5, no. 3 (1992), 438.

29. Byerly, *Fever of War,* 24, 37; Bristow, "'It's as Bad as Anything Can Be,'" 136; John S. Billings, *Progress of Medicine in the Nineteenth Century,* in *The Smithsonian Report for 1900* (Washington, DC: Government Printing Office, 1901), 643.

II: DISEASES OF WAR

1. Philip Jenkins, *The Great and Holy War: How World War I Became a Religious Crusade* (San Francisco: HarperOne, 2014), 29, 48; Modris Eksteins, *Rites of Spring: The Great War and the Birth of the Modern Age* (Boston: Houghton Mifflin, 1989), 99.

2. German writer Kurt Tucholsky, quoted in "First World War: 15 Legacies Still with Us Today," *The Guardian,* January 15, 2014, www.theguardian.com/world/2014/jan/15 /firstworldwar.

3. Crosby, *America's Forgotten Pandemic,* 17; Emmanuel Bourcier, "The Gas Attack," *Current History,* September 1916, jfredmacdonald.com/worldwarone1914-1918/battles-18gas-attack .html.

4. Juliet Nicolson, *The Great Silence: Britain from the Shadow of the First World War to the Dawn of the Jazz Age* (New York: Grove Press, 2009), 21; Eksteins, *Rites of Spring,* 148.

5. Eksteins, *Rites of Spring,* 146–147.

6. Keen, "Military Surgery in 1861 and 1918," 16.

7. Eksteins, *Rites of Spring,* 152, 153.

8. Ibid., 146, 147.

9. Ibid., 149; Hanson, *Unknown Soldiers,* 33.

10. Hanson, *Unknown Soldiers,* 40; "Trench Rats," Spartacus Educational, spartacus-educational. com/FWWrats.htm.

11. Eksteins, *Rites of Spring,* 150–151.

12. Johnathon E. Briggs, "Wrights Saw Airplanes as Tools of Peace," *Baltimore Sun,* April 20, 2003, www.baltimoresun.com/news/bal-wrights05-story.html.

13. Lyn Macdonald, *Somme* (London: Michael Joseph, 1983), 209; Eksteins, *Rites of Spring,* 153.

14. Eksteins, *Rites of Spring,* 152; Richard Rhodes, *Masters of Death: The SS-Einsatzgruppen and the Invention of the Holocaust* (New York: Knopf, 2002), 31, 32.

15. Nicolson, *The Great Silence,* 64.

16. Jenkins, *The Great and Holy War,* 48–49.

17. Bourcier, "The Gas Attack."

18. Jennifer D. Keene, "Americans at War: Assessing the Significance of American Participation in the Great War," in *New Zealand's Great War,* ed. John Crawford and I. C. McGibbon, 108–122 (Auckland, New Zealand: Exisle Publishing, 2007), 119–120, www.chapman.edu /our-faculty/files/publications/keene-jennifer/Americans%20at%20War.pdf.

19. www.nps.gov/vafo. In the Mexican War (1846–1848), seven American soldiers died of disease for each one killed by the enemy.

20. Russ Hatter, "Disease Killed More Soldiers Than Combat," *Civil War RX* (blog), September 25, 2011, www.civilwarrx.blogspot.com/2015/08/disease-killed-more-soldiers-than -combat.html; Matthew R. Smallman-Raynor and Andrew D. Cliff, "Impact of Infectious

Diseases on War," *Infectious Disease Clinics of North America,* 18 (2004), 354; James I. Robertson Jr., *Soldiers Blue and Gray* (Columbia: University of South Carolina Press, 1988), 145–169.

21. Byerly, *Fever of War,* 39.

22. Victor C. Vaughan, *A Doctor's Memories* (Indianapolis: Bobbs-Merrill, 1926), 198–199.

23. Ibid., 198.

24. Byerly, *Fever of War,* 46, 47.

25. Ibid., 9.

26. William Osler, *The Evolution of Modern Medicine: A Series of Lectures Delivered at Yale University on the Silliman Foundation, in April, 1913* (New Haven, CT: Yale University Press, 1921), www.gutenberg.org/files/1566/1566-h/1566-h.htm.

27. Dorothy H. Crawford, *The Invisible Enemy: A Natural History of Viruses* (New York: Oxford University Press, 2000), 8.

28. Quoted in Cristina Luiggi, "Same Poop, Different Gut," *The Scientist,* November 3, 2010, www.the-scientist.com/?articles.view/articleNo/29352/title/Same-poop-different-gut/.

29. Crawford, *The Invisible Enemy,* 7–8.

30. Ibid., 6.

31. "Viruses," *Encyclopedia of Life,* www.eol.org; Carl Zimmer, *A Planet of Viruses* (Chicago: University of Chicago Press, 2011), 42.

32. Barry, *The Great Influenza,* 100.

33. Pettit and Bailie, *A Cruel Wind,* 33.

34. Barry, *The Great Influenza,* 104.

35. Lynette Iezzoni, *Influenza 1918: The Worst Epidemic in American History* (New York: TV Books, 1999), 111.

36. Nicolson, *The Great Silence,* 26–27; Mark Honigsbaum, *Living with Enza: The Forgotten Story of Britain and the Great Flu Pandemic of 1918* (London: Macmillan, 2009), 36.

37. William Mulligan, *The Great War for Peace* (New Haven, CT: Yale University Press, 2014), 251.

38. Pete Davies, *Catching Cold: The Hunt for a Killer Virus* (New York: Penguin Books, 2000), 53–54, 56.

39. Barry, *The Great Influenza,* 169–171.

40. Honigsbaum, *Living with Enza,* 18.

41. Ibid., 29–30.

42. Davies, *Catching Cold,* 108; Nicolas Mignon, "The 'Spanish' Flu Hits Belgium," RTBF, www.rtbf.be/ww1/topics/detail_the-spanish-flu-hits-belgium-1918-1919?id=8358615.

43. "Spanish Influenza Is Raging in the German Army," *New York Times,* June 27, 1918.

44. Erich von Ludendorff, *Ludendorff's Own Story, August 1914–November 1918: The Great War from the Siege of Liège to the Signing of the Armistice as Viewed from the Grand Headquarters of the German Army,* 2 vols. in one (1919; repr., Cranbury, NJ: Scholars Bookshelf, 2006), vol. 2; Alexander Watson, *Ring of Steel: Germany and Austria-Hungary at War, 1914–1918* (New York: Penguin Books, 2015), 528.

45. Pettit and Bailie, *A Cruel Wind,* 72.

46. Antonio Trilla, "The 1918 'Spanish Flu' in Spain," *Clinical Infectious Diseases,* 47, no. 5 (2008), 668–673, cid.oxfordjournals.org/content/47/5/668.full.pdf+html.

47. Barry, *The Great Influenza,* 172.

48. Krystal Rose, "Called to Death: A Case Study on the 1918 Influenza Pandemic in Coles County, Illinois," *Historia,* 17 (2008), www.eiu.edu/historia/Historia2008Rose.pdf.

49. Herbert French, "The Clinical Features of the Influenza Epidemic of 1918–19," in Ministry of Health of Great Britain, *Report on the Pandemic of Influenza, 1918–19* (London: His Majesty's Stationery Office, 1920), 68.

50. Barry, *The Great Influenza,* 174.

III: PUNY MAN: DROWNING IN THE SECOND WAVE

1. Crosby, *America's Forgotten Pandemic,* 39.

2. Ibid., 40.

3. Pettit and Bailie, *A Cruel Wind,* 85–86.

4. Crosby, *America's Forgotten Pandemic,* 4.

5. John N. Bombardt Jr. and Heidi E. Brown, *Potential Influenza Effects on Military Populations,* IDA Paper P-3786 (Alexandria, VA: Institute for Defense Analyses, December 2003), 12; Crosby, *America's Forgotten Pandemic,* 5; Honigsbaum, *Living with Enza,* 72; Byerly, *Fever of War,* 74–75.

6. Crosby, *America's Forgotten Pandemic,* 8; Davies, *Catching Cold,* 62.

7. David S. Fedson, "Was Bacterial Pneumonia the Predominant Cause of Death in the 1918–1919 Influenza Pandemic?," *Journal of Infectious Diseases,* 199, no. 9 (2009), 1408–1409, jid.oxfordjournals.org/content/199/9/1408.full.

8. Roy Grist, "Flu Epidemic of 1918," Digital History, www.digitalhistory.uh.edu/disp_textbook.cfm?smtID=3&psid=1112.

9. Ibid.

10. Vaughan, *A Doctor's Memories,* 199.

11. Kolata, *Flu,* 16.

12. Simon Flexner and James Thomas Flexner, *William Henry Welch and the Heroic Age of American Medicine* (New York: Viking Press, 1941), 376; Honigsbaum, *Living with Enza,* 72.

13. Centers for Disease Control and Prevention, *Pandemic Influenza—Past, Present, Future: Communicating Today Based on the Lessons from the 1918–1919 Influenza Pandemic; Workshop Proceedings,* October 17, 2006, www.flu.gov/pandemic/workshop.pdf; Flexner and Flexner, *William Henry Welch,* 376–377.

14. Pettit and Bailie, *A Cruel Wind,* 172; Centers for Disease Control and Prevention, *Pandemic Influenza,* 5; Iezzoni, *Influenza 1918,* 120–121.

15. Barry, *The Great Influenza,* 239; Kolata, *Flu,* 5.

16. Byerly, "The U.S. Military and the Influenza Pandemic of 1918–1919."

17. Rachel Wedeking, "Oral History with Ms. Josie Mabel Brown" (Washington, DC: Office of Medical History, Bureau of Medicine and Surgery, 1986), www.med.navy.mil/.bumed /nmhistory/Oral%20Histories2/BROWN%20Josie%20%Mabel.pdf.

18. Ibid.; Ron Grossman, "1918 Influenza Epidemic Struck Hard, Fast," *Chicago Tribune,* October 18, 2014, www.chicagotribune.com/news/ct-epidemic-scare-flashback-1019-2 -20141018-story.html.

19. Peter C. Wever and Leo van Bergen, "Death from 1918 Pandemic Influenza During the First World War: A Perspective from Personal and Anecdotal Evidence," *Influenza and Other Respiratory Viruses,* 8, no. 5 (September 2014), 536–546.

20. Johnson and Mueller, "Updating the Accounts," 111; Barry, *The Great Influenza,* 361.

21. Barry, *The Great Influenza,* 363; Johnson and Mueller, "Updating the Accounts," 111.

22. Larry Smith, "A Hurricane Across the Green Fields of Life: How the 1918 Flu Affected the Caribbean," Bahama Pundit, October 26, 2005, www.bahamapundit.com/2005/10/how _the_1918_fl_1.html; David Killingray, "The Influenza Pandemic of 1918–1919 in the British Caribbean," *Social History of Medicine,* 7, no. 1 (April 1994), 59–87, www.ncbi.nlm.nih.gov /pubmed/11639296.

23. Smith, "A Hurricane Across the Green Fields of Life"; Killingray, "The Influenza Pandemic of 1918–1919 in the British Caribbean."

24. Trevor Wilson, *The Myriad Faces of War: Britain and the Great War, 1914–1918* (Cambridge, England: Polity Press, 1986), 650, 652; Richard Collier, *The Plague of the Spanish Lady: The Influenza Pandemic of 1918–1919* (New York: Atheneum, 1974), 83; John Toland, *No Man's Land: 1918, the Last Year of the Great War* (Garden City, NY: Doubleday, 1980), 299.

25. Patricia Marsh, "'Mysterious Malady Spreading': Press Coverage of the 1918–19 Influenza Pandemic in Ireland," *Quest Proceedings of the QUB AHSS Conference June 2008,* 6 (Autumn 2008), 169, 171, www.qub.ac/uk/quest.

26. Johnson and Mueller, "Updating the Accounts," 111, 113; Toland, *No Man's Land,* 498–499; Trilla, "The 1918 'Spanish Flu' in Spain"; img.medscape.com/article/703/354/703354-tab1.jpg.

27. Howard Phillips, "Influenza Pandemic," *International Encyclopedia of the First World War,* encyclopedia.1914-1918-online.net/article/influenza_pandemic.

28. Ibid.

29. Barry, *The Great Influenza,* 363; Killingray, "The Influenza Pandemic of 1918–1919 in the British Caribbean," 34.

30. Barry, *The Great Influenza,* 363; Johnson and Mueller, "Updating the Accounts," 110.

31. Killingray, "The Influenza Pandemic of 1918–1919 in the British Caribbean," 77; Honigsbaum, *Living with Enza,* 146.

32. Howard Phillips, "Influenza Pandemic (Africa)," *International Encyclopedia of the First World War,* encyclopedia.1914-1918-online.net/article/influenza_pandemic_africa; Johnson and Mueller, "Updating the Accounts," 110.

33. Phillips, "Influenza Pandemic (Africa)"; Johnson and Mueller, "Updating the Accounts," 110.

34. Howard Phillips, "Why Did It Happen? Religious Explanations of the 'Spanish' Flu Epidemic in South Africa," *Historically Speaking,* 9, no. 7 (September–October 2008), 34.

35. Phillips, "Influenza Pandemic."

36. Ibid.

37. Bhagavad Gita, chapter 11, verses 31–33.

38. A. A. Hoehling, *The Great Epidemic* (Boston: Little, Brown, 1961), 108.

39. Ibid., 109; Johnson and Mueller, "Updating the Accounts," 112.

40. Johnson and Mueller, "Updating the Accounts," 112.

41. Ibid.; Barry, *The Great Influenza,* 333.

42. Johnson and Mueller, "Updating the Accounts," 114; Hoehling, *The Great Epidemic,* 109–110; Barry, *The Great Influenza,* 364.

43. Phillips, "Influenza Pandemic."

44. Barry, *The Great Influenza,* 365.

IV: A FEAR AND PANIC: INFLUENZA AND AMERICAN SOCIETY

1. Hoehling, *The Great Epidemic,* 119–120; Crosby, *America's Forgotten Pandemic,* 11; Collier, *The Plague of the Spanish Lady,* 183.

2. Crosby, *America's Forgotten Pandemic,* 264.

3. Alan M. Kraut, "Immigration, Ethnicity, and the Pandemic," *Public Health Reports,* vol. 125, Supplement 3 (2010): "Influenza Pandemic in the United States," 130, www.ncbi.nih.gov/pmc/articles/PMC2862341.

4. Ibid., 125, 128.

5. Centers for Disease Control and Prevention, *Pandemic Influenza,* 6.

6. George Bedborough, *Arms and the Clergy, 1914–1918* (London: Pioneer Press, 1934), 21.

7. David T. Morgan, "The Revivalist as Patriot: Billy Sunday and World War I," *Journal of Presbyterian History (1962–1985),* 51, no. 2 (Summer 1973), 203, 209; Frederick C. Giffin, "Billy Sunday: The Evangelist as 'Patriot,'" *Social Science,* 48, no. 4 (Autumn 1973), 220; Joseph E.

Persico, "The Great Swine Flu Epidemic of 1918," *American Heritage Magazine,* 27, no. 4 (June 1976), www.americanheritage.com/print/53422.

8. Christine M. Kreiser, "1918 Spanish Influenza Outbreak: The Enemy Within," History Net, October 27, 2006, www.historynet.com/1918-spanish-influenza-outbreak-the-enemy-within .htm; Crosby, *America's Forgotten Pandemic,* 216.

9. Iezzoni, *Influenza 1918,* 67.

10. "Think Influenza Came in U-Boat," *New York Times,* September 19, 1918.

11. Collier, *The Plague of the Spanish Lady,* 166–167; Persico, "The Great Swine Flu Epidemic of 1918"; Pettit and Bailie, *A Cruel Wind,* 189; Barry, *The Great Influenza,* 343.

12. Crosby, *America's Forgotten Pandemic,* 74.

13. Pettit and Bailie, *A Cruel Wind,* 131.

14. Richard Koszarski, "Flu Season: *Moving Picture World* Reports on Pandemic Influenza, 1918–19," *Film History,* 17, no. 4 (2005), 469.

15. Stephen J. Leonard, "The 1918 Influenza Outbreak: An Unforgettable Legacy," *Denver Post,* May 3, 2009; Barry, *The Great Influenza,* 345; Julian A. Navarro, "Influenza in 1918: An Epidemic in Images," *Public Health Reports,* vol. 125, Supplement 3 (2010): "Influenza Pandemic in the United States," 12, www.ncbi.nih.gov/pmc/articles/PMC2862330.

16. Collier, *The Plague of the Spanish Lady,* 76; Iezzoni, *Influenza 1918,* 141–142.

17. Tom Quinn, *Flu: A Social History of Influenza* (London: New Holland Publishers, 2008), 141; Collier, *The Plague of the Spanish Lady,* 77.

18. Hoehling, *The Great Epidemic,* 62, 81; Kirsty Duncan, *Hunting the 1918 Flu* (Toronto: University of Toronto Press, 2003), 12; Kenneth A. White, "Pittsburgh in the Great Epidemic of 1918," *Western Pennsylvania Historical Magazine,* 68, no. 3 (July 1985), 227.

19. Nancy Tomes, "'Destroyer and Teacher': Managing the Masses During the 1918–1919 Influenza Pandemic," *Public Health Reports,* vol. 125, Supplement 3 (2010): "Influenza Pandemic in the United States," 55, www.ncbi.nih.gov/pmc/articles/PMC2862334; "Experts Disagree on Epidemic Here," *New York Times,* October 7, 1918.

20. Leonard, "The 1918 Influenza Outbreak"; Collier, *The Plague of the Spanish Lady,* 194.

21. Iezzoni, *Influenza 1918,* 128; Barry, *The Great Influenza,* 350.

22. Collier, *The Plague of the Spanish Lady,* 193, 194; Hoehling, *The Great Epidemic,* 161; Iezzoni, *Influenza 1918,* 84, 161.

23. Crosby, *America's Forgotten Pandemic,* 102; Kirsten Moore, "Medical Manipulation: Public Health as a Political Tool in the 1918–19 Influenza Epidemic in San Francisco," *Voces Novae,* 3, no. 1 (2011), journals.chapman.edu/ojs/index.php/VocesNovae/article/view/212/545.

24. Leonard, "The 1918 Influenza Outbreak"; Hoehling, *The Great Epidemic,* 101, 103; Centers for Disease Control and Prevention, *Pandemic Influenza,* 7.

25. French, "The Clinical Features of the Influenza Epidemic of 1918–19," 92–93.

26. "New York Prepared for Influenza Siege," *New York Times,* September 19, 1918.

27. White, "Pittsburgh in the Great Epidemic of 1918," 225.

28. Barry, *The Great Influenza,* 355; Eileen A. Lynch, "The Flu of 1918," *Pennsylvania Gazette,* November–December 1998, www.upenn.edu/gazette/1198/lynch/htm; Davies, *Catching Cold,* 92; imageO-rubylane.s3.amazonaws.com.shops.ctyankeeantiques/25-0430B.2L.jpg?45.

29. Collier, *The Plague of the Spanish Lady,* 198; Iezzoni, *Influenza 1918,* 73, 119; Sarah Cummings, "Spanish Influenza Outbreak, 1918," International World History Project, history-world.org /spanish_influenza_of_1918.htm.

30. Hoehling, *The Great Epidemic,* 72.

31. Persico, "The Great Swine Flu Epidemic of 1918."

32. Ibid.; Hoehling, *The Great Epidemic,* 135; Lynch, "The Flu of 1918."

33. Lynch, "The Flu of 1918"; Pettit and Bailie, *A Cruel Wind,* 111.

34. Iezzoni, *Influenza 1918,* 134, 135.

35. Davies, *Catching Cold,* 84; Barry, *The Great Influenza,* 132; Iezzoni, *Influenza 1918,* 148.

36. Iezzoni, *Influenza 1918,* 148, 149; Crosby, *America's Forgotten Pandemic,* 83.

37. Hoehling, *The Great Epidemic,* 147.

38. Ibid., 90.

39. "Spanish Influenza Much like Grippe," *New York Times,* September 22, 1918; White, "Pittsburgh in the Great Epidemic of 1918," 236.

40. Iezzoni, *Influenza 1918,* 84; Kolata, *Flu,* 53; Davies, *Catching Cold,* 86.

41. Alexandra Minna Stern et al., " 'Better Off in School': School Medical Inspection as a Public Health Strategy During the 1918–1919 Influenza Pandemic in the United States," *Public Health Reports,* vol. 125, Supplement 3 (2010): "Influenza Pandemic in the United States," 64, www.ncbi.nih.gov/pmc/articles/PMC2862335.

42. Collier, *The Plague of the Spanish Lady,* 157; Stern, " 'Better Off in School,' " 67.

43. Stern, " 'Better Off in School,' " 67.

44. Kraut, "Immigration, Ethnicity, and the Pandemic," 129.

45. Iezzoni, *Influenza 1918,* 66.

46. "The Great Pandemic: The United States in 1918–1919," www.flu.gov/pandemic/history/1918 /your_state/southeast/dc; Iezzoni, *Influenza 1918,* 154–155.

47. Iezzoni, *Influenza 1918,* 120.

48. Francis Russell, "A Journal of the Plague: The 1918 Influenza," in *The Great Interlude: Neglected Events and Persons from the First World War to the Depression* (New York: McGraw-Hill, 1964), 37.

49. Bristow, " 'It's as Bad as Anything Can Be,' " 139.

50. Laurie Garrett, "The Next Pandemic?" *Foreign Affairs,* July–August 2005, www.foreignaffairs.com/articles/2005-07-01-next-pandemic; Pettit and Bailie, *A Cruel Wind,* 149; Iezzoni, *Influenza 1918,* 272.

51. Phillips, "Influenza Pandemic."

52. Iezzoni, *Influenza 1918,* 157; Edward Robb Ellis, *Echoes of Distant Thunder: Life in the United States, 1914–1918* (New York: Coward, McCann & Geoghegan, 1975), 468–469.

53. Barry, *The Great Influenza,* 348; Hoehling, *The Great Epidemic,* 115; Lynch, "The Flu of 1918"; Quinn, *Flu,* 145.

54. Barry, *The Great Influenza,* 339–340; Pettit and Bailie, *A Cruel Wind,* 43.

55. Byerly, "The U.S. Military and the Influenza Pandemic of 1918–1919"; Collier, *The Plague of the Spanish Lady,* 102, 103.

56. Collier, *The Plague of the Spanish Lady,* 170.

57. Ibid., 195; Barry, *The Great Influenza,* 342.

58. White, "Pittsburgh in the Great Epidemic of 1918," 229; Hoehling, *The Great Epidemic,* 62; "Influenza 1918," *American Experience,* complete program transcript, PBS, www.pbs.org/wgbh /americanexperience/features/transcript/influenza-transcript.

59. Crosby, *America's Forgotten Pandemic,* 51.

60. Ibid., 7.

61. Barry, *The Great Influenza,* 142.

62. Arlene W. Keeling, "'Alert to the Necessities of the Emergency': U.S. Nursing During the 1918 Influenza Pandemic," *Public Health Reports,* vol. 125, Supplement 3 (2010): "Influenza Pandemic in the United States," 109, www.ncbi.nih.gov/pmc/articles/PMC2862339.

63. Dorothy Deming, "Influenza—1918: Reliving the Great Epidemic," *American Journal of Nursing,* 57, no. 10 (October 1957), 1309.

64. Kraut, "Immigration, Ethnicity, and the Pandemic," 128; Miles Ott et al., "Lessons Learned from the 1918–1919 Influenza Pandemic in Minneapolis and St. Paul, Minnesota," *Public Health Reports,* 122, no. 6 (November–December 2007), 804, www.ncbi.nlm.nih.gov/pmc /articles/PMC1997248.

65. Deming, "Influenza—1918," 1309.

66. Iezzoni, *Influenza 1918,* 123–124.

67. Hoehling, *The Great Epidemic,* 98; "Asks Experts' Aid to Check Epidemic," *New York Times,* October 13, 1918.

68. Hoehling, *The Great Epidemic,* 98.

V: TO THE BITTER END

1. Byerly, *Fever of War,* 108.

2. Ibid., 109.

3. Crosby, *America's Forgotten Pandemic,* 165–166.

4. Thomas Fleming, *The Illusion of Victory: America in World War I* (New York: Basic Books, 2004), 118–119.

5. Ibid., 305.

6. Byerly, *Fever of War,* 114; John J. Pershing, *My Experiences in the World War,* 2 vols. (New York: Frederick A. Stokes Co., 1931), 2:327; Gregor Dallas, *1918: War and Peace* (New York: Overlook Press, 2001), 100.

7. Byerly, *Fever of War,* 118.

8. David McCullough, *Truman* (New York: Simon & Schuster, 1992), 136.

9. David W. Tschanz, "Plague of the Spanish Lady," MilitaryHistoryOnline.com, December 11, 2011, www.militaryhistoryonline.com/wwi/articles/plagueofspanishlady.aspx.

10. Lyn Macdonald, *The Roses of No Man's Land* (New York: Atheneum, 1989), 287, 288.

11. Ibid., 284–285.

12. Ralph Raico, "The Blockade and Attempted Starvation of Germany," Mises Daily, May 7, 2010, mises.org/library/blockade-and-attempted-starvation-germany.

13. Tschanz, "Plague of the Spanish Lady."

14. Ibid.; David Clay Large, *Berlin* (New York: Basic Books, 2000), 133–134.

15. Peter Loewenberg, "Psychohistorical Origins of the Nazi Youth Cohort," *American Historical Review,* 76, no. 5 (December 1971), 1457–1502, www.history.ucsb.edu/faculty/marcuse /classes/201/articles/71LoewenbergOriginsNaziYouthCohortAHR.pdf, 1473, 1477.

16. Pettit and Bailie, *A Cruel Wind,* 74; Tschanz, "Plague of the Spanish Lady"; Richard M. Watt, *The Kings Depart: The Tragedy of Germany; Versailles and the German Revolution* (New York: Simon & Schuster, 1968), 150; Toland, *No Man's Land,* 499; Raico, "The Blockade and Attempted Starvation of Germany."

17. Bombardt and Brown, *Potential Influenza Effects on Military Populations,* 14; Crosby, *America's Forgotten Pandemic,* 71, 160.

18. Byerly, "The U.S. Military and the Influenza Pandemic of 1918–1919"; Crosby, *America's Forgotten Pandemic,* 49.

19. Collier, *The Plague of the Spanish Lady,* 73.

20. Barry, *The Great Influenza,* 307. Italics added.

21. Ibid., 307.

22. Collier, *The Plague of the Spanish Lady,* 75.

23. David M. Kennedy, *Over Here: The First World War and American Society* (New York: Oxford University Press, 1980), 189.

24. Bristow, "'It's as Bad as Anything Can Be,'" 136; Crosby, *America's Forgotten Pandemic,* 129.

25. Crosby, *America's Forgotten Pandemic,* 127; Hoehling, *The Great Epidemic,* 39; Honigsbaum, *Living with Enza,* 73.

26. Crosby, *America's Forgotten Pandemic,* 131–132.

27. Ibid., 133; Honigsbaum, *Living with Enza,* 74.

28. Persico, "The Great Swine Flu Epidemic of 1918"; "Armistice—the End of World War I, 1918," EyeWitness to History, 2004, www.eyewitnesstohistory.com/armistice.htm; C. N. Trueman, "November 11th 1918," History Learning Site, March 6, 2015, www.historylearningsite.co.uk/world-war-one/november-11th-1918.

29. McCullough, *Truman,* 134; Persico, *Eleventh Month, Eleventh Day, Eleventh Hour,* 354, 364; "When This Lousy War Is Over," World War One Photos, www.ww1photos.com /WhenThisLousyWarIsOver.html.

30. Dallas, *1918,* 120–121; Martin Gilbert, *The First World War: A Complete History* (New York: Henry Holt, 1994), 501.

31. Collier, *The Plague of the Spanish Lady,* 235.

32. Persico, *Eleventh Month, Eleventh Day, Eleventh Hour,* 364, 366, 369.

33. Ibid., 364; Quinn, *Flu,* 148; Dallas, *1918,* 199.

34. Pettit and Bailie, *A Cruel Wind,* 145.

35. A. Scott Berg, *Wilson* (New York: G. P. Putnam's Sons, 2013), 583.

36. Margaret MacMillan, *Peacemakers: The Paris Conference of 1919 and Its Attempt to End War* (London: John Murray, 2001), 14; Fleming, *The Illusion of Victory,* 321.

37. Crosby, *America's Forgotten Pandemic,* 172.

38. Honigsbaum, *Living with Enza,* 133.

39. Ibid.; Crosby, *America's Forgotten Pandemic,* 181; Iezzoni, *Influenza 1918,* 188.

40. Pettit and Bailie, *A Cruel Wind,* 161; Dallas, *1918,* 424.

41. Thomas A. Bailey, *Wilson and the Peacemakers,* 2 vols. in one (New York: Macmillan, 1947), 1:221.

42. Arthur Walworth, *Woodrow Wilson,* 2 vols. in one (New York: Longmans, Green, 1958), 2:297n13; Honigsbaum, *Living with Enza,* 138; Crosby, *America's Forgotten Pandemic,* 191, 192.

43. MacMillan, *Peacemakers,* 489.

44. Iezzoni, *Influenza 1918,* 182.

45. Barry, *The Great Influenza,* 370–371.

46. Jeffery K. Taubenberger et al., "Reconstruction of the 1918 Influenza Virus: Unexpected Rewards from the Past," *mBio,* 3, no. 5 (September 11, 2012), e0020–212, mbio.asm.org /content/3/5/e00201-12.full.pdf.

47. Barry, *The Great Influenza,* 392; Collier, *The Plague of the Spanish Lady,* 178–179; Pettit and Bailie, *A Cruel Wind,* 29–30; Honigsbaum, *Living with Enza,* 142–143.

VI: A DETECTIVE STORY

1. Crosby, *America's Forgotten Pandemic,* 314.

2. Vaughan, *A Doctor's Memories,* 432; Flexner and Flexner, *William Henry Welch,* 376–377.

3. Hoehling, *The Great Epidemic,* 194.

4. John M. Eyler, "The State of Science, Microbiology, and Vaccines Circa 1918," *Public Health Reports,* vol. 125, Supplement 3 (2010): "Influenza Pandemic in the United States," 27–36, www.ncbi.nih.gov/pmc/articles/PMC286332.

5. Collier, *The Plague of the Spanish Lady,* 141, 142.

6. Eyler, "The State of Science, Microbiology, and Vaccines Circa 1918."

7. Crosby, *America's Forgotten Pandemic,* 288, 289; Barbara C. Canavan, "Collaboration Across the Pond: Influenza Virus Research, Interwar United States and Britain," Rockefeller Archive Center Research Reports, December 31, 2014, 3–4, www.rockarch.org/publications/resrep /canavan.pdf.

8. Malcolm Gladwell, "The Dead Zone," *The New Yorker,* September 29, 1997, 52, gladwell.com /the-dead-zone.

9. Davies, *Catching Cold,* 257.

10. Ibid., 255.

11. Ibid., 229.

12. "1918 Spanish Flu Epidemic," Alaska Web, alaskaweb.org/disease/1918flu.htm.

13. Davies, *Catching Cold,* 114; "1918 Spanish Flu Epidemic."

14. Davies, *Catching Cold,* 226, 235–236.

15. Ibid., 236.

16. Ibid., 253–254.

17. "1918 Spanish Flu Epidemic"; David Brown, "Resurrecting 1918 Flu Virus Took Many Turns," *Washington Post,* October 10, 2005, www.washingtonpost.com/wp-dyn/content /article/2005/10/09/AR2005100900932_pf.html.

18. Jeffery K. Taubenberger, "Jeffery Taubenberger—Full Transcript," Conversations with Pathologists, interview, November 27, 2007, www.pathsoc.org/conversations/index.php ?view=article&catid=65%3Ajeffery-taubenberger&id=92%3Ajeffery-taubenberger-full -transcript&option=com_content.

19. Elizabeth Fernandez, "The Virus Detective: Dr. John Hultin Has Found Evidence of the 1918 Flu Epidemic That Has Eluded Experts for Decades," *San Francisco Chronicle,* February 17, 2002, www.sfgate.com/magazine/article/The-Virus-detective-Dr-John-Hultin -has-found-2872017.php.

20. Centers for Disease Control and Prevention, "We Heard the Bells: The Influenza of 1918," www.flu.gov/pandemic/history/weheardthebells/script_120709.html.

21. Ibid.

22. Fernandez, "The Virus Detective"; Brown, "Resurrecting 1918 Flu Virus Took Many Turns."

23. Kolata, *Flu,* 264–265; Centers for Disease Control and Prevention, "We Heard the Bells."

24. Taubenberger, "Jeffery Taubenberger—Full Transcript."

25. Michael Specter, "Nature's Bioterrorist," *The New Yorker,* February 28, 2005, www.newyorker
    .com/magazine/2005/02/28/natures-bioterrorist-2.

26. Quinn, *Flu,* 176–177, 183; Davies, *Catching Cold,* 27–28; Pettit and Bailie, *A Cruel Wind,*
    238–239; Jeffery K. Taubenberger and David M. Morens, "1918 Influenza: The Mother of
    All Pandemics," *Emerging Infectious Diseases,* 12, no. 1 (January 2006), www.cdc.gov/eid
    /article/12/1/05-0979_article.

27. Andrew Nikiforuk, *Pandemonium: Bird Flu, Mad Cow Disease and Other Biological Plagues of
    the 21st Century* (Toronto: Viking Canada, 2006), 19.

28. Ibid., 6, 23.

29. Ibid., 1.

30. Ibid., 2–3, 23.

31. Specter, "Nature's Bioterrorist."

32. Laurie Garrett, "The Bioterrorist Next Door," *Foreign Policy,* December 15, 2011,
    foreignpolicy.com/2011/12/15/the-bioterrorist-next-door.

33. Nikiforuk, *Pandemonium,* 15; Specter, "Nature's Bioterrorist."

34. "Worst U.S. Bird Flu Outbreak in History Expands to Michigan," Reuters, June 8, 2015,
    www.reuters.com/article/us-health-birdflu-michigan-idUSKBN0OO29S20150608.

35. Tomes, " 'Destroyer and Teacher,' " 60; Tomes, "The Making of a Germ Panic, Then and
    Now," 191–198.

36. Specter, "Nature's Bioterrorist."

37. "CONPLAN 3551-09, March 22, 2009," Government Attic, governmentattic.org.

38. Osterholm, "Preparing for the Next Pandemic," 31–33.

39. Michael Specter, "The Deadliest Virus," *The New Yorker,* March 12, 2012, www.newyorker
    .com/magazine/2012/03/12/the-deadliest-virus.

40. Garrett, "The Bioterrorist Next Door."

41. Denise Grady and Donald G. McNeil Jr., "Debate Persists on Deadly Flu Made Airborne,"
    New York Times, December 26, 2011, www.nytimes.com/2011/12/27/science/debate-persists-on
    -deadly-flu-made-airborne.html?_r=0.

42. Ibid.

43. Steve Connor, "Exclusive: Controversial US Scientist Creates Deadly New Flu Strain
    for Pandemic Research," *The Independent,* June 30, 2014, www.independent.co.uk/news
    /science/exclusive-controversial-us-scientist-creates-deadly-new-flu-strain-for-pandemic
    -research-9577088.html.

44. Ian Sample, "Scientists Condemn 'Crazy, Dangerous' Creation of Deadly Airborne
    Flu Virus," *The Guardian,* June 11, 2014, www.theguardian.com/science/2014/jun/11
    /crazy-dangerous-creation-deadly-airborne-flu-virus.

45. Specter, "The Deadliest Virus."

46. Cassandra Willyard, "Behind the Steel Door," The Last Word on Nothing, February 11, 2015, www.lastwordonnothing.com/2015/02/11/behind-the-steel-door.

47. "Contemporary Islamist Ideology Authorizing Genocidal Murder," Middle East Media Research Institute, Special Report no. 25, January 27, 2004, www.memri.org/report /en/0/0/0/0/0/0/0/1049.htm; David Aaron, *In Their Own Words: Voices of Jihad—Compilation and Commentary* (Santa Monica, CA: RAND Corp., 2008), 154, 171; Carl J. Ciovacco, "The Erosion of Non-combatant Immunity Within Al Qaeda," Small Wars Journal, smallwarsjournal.com/blog/journal/docs-temp/67-ciovacco.pdf; Jonathan D. Halevi, "Al-Qaeda's Intellectual Legacy: New Radical Islamic Thinking Justifying Genocide of Infidels," *Jerusalem Viewpoints,* December 1, 2003, www.jcpa.org/jl/vp508.htm.

48. "Contemporary Islamist Ideology Authorizing Genocidal Murder"; Anne Speckhard, "The New Global Jihad, 9-11, and the Use of Weapons of Mass Destruction: Changes in Mindset and Modus Operandi," theclaw.typepad.com.speckhard_vault/files/Al_Qaeda.pdf.

49. Specter, "The Deadliest Virus"; Garrett, "The Bioterrorist Next Door."

50. Alicia Lu, "Why Publishing a Bird Flu–Human Transmission Guide Was an Incredibly Dumb Idea," *Bustle,* April 11, 2014, www.bustle.com/articles/20893-why-publishing-a-bird-flu -human-transmission-guide-was-an-incredibly-dumb-idea.

51. Nikiforuk, *Pandemonium,* 17, 18.

52. Pettit and Bailie, *A Cruel Wind,* 250.

FURTHER READING

"1918 Spanish Influenza Epidemic." Alaska Web. alaskaweb.org/disease/1918flu.htm.

Alcabes, Philip. "The Bioterrorism Scare." *The American Scholar,* 73, no. 2 (Spring 2004), 35–45.

The American Influenza Epidemic of 1918–1919: A Digital Encyclopedia. www.influenzaarchive.org /about.html.

Appenzeller, Tim. "Tracking the Next Killer Flu." *National Geographic,* October 2005. ngm /nationalgeographic.com/ngm/0510/feature1.

Association of Schools of Public Health. "Sure Cures for Influenza, November 8, 1918." *Public Health Reports (1896–1970),* 33, no. 45 (November 8, 1918), 1931–1933.

Baker, Robert. *Epidemic! The Past, Present, and Future of the Diseases That Made Us.* London: Vision Paperbacks, 2007.

Barker, Clyde F. "Thomas Eakins and His Medical Clinics." *Proceedings of the American Philosophical Society,* 153, no. 1 (March 2009), 1–47.

Barry, John M. *The Great Influenza: The Epic Story of the Deadliest Plague in History.* New York: Viking Penguin, 2004.

———. "What the 1918 Flu Pandemic Teaches Us." *MLO,* 38, no. 9 (September 2006), 26–27. www.mlo-online.com.

Bayne-Jones, Stanhope. "Immunologists During the First World War: One Soldier-Scientist's Experience." *AAI Newsletter,* December 2012, 16–23. www.aai.org/About/History/Articles /AAI_History_008.pdf.

Berg, A. Scott. *Wilson.* New York: G. P. Putnam's Sons, 2013.

Bombardt, John N., Jr., and Heidi E. Brown. *Potential Influenza Effects on Military Populations.* IDA Paper P-3786. Alexandria, VA: Institute for Defense Analyses, December 2003.

Bray, R. S. *Armies of Pestilence: The Impact of Disease on History.* New York: Barnes & Noble, 2000.

Bristow, Nancy K. "'It's as Bad as Anything Can Be': Patients, Identity, and the Influenza Pandemic." *Public Health Reports,* vol. 125, Supplement 3 (2010): "Influenza Pandemic in the United States," 134–144. www.ncbi.nih.gov/pmc/articles/PMC2862342.

Byerly, Carol R. *Fever of War: The Influenza Epidemic and the U.S. Army During World War I.* New York: New York University Press, 2005.

―――. "The U.S. Military and the Influenza Pandemic of 1918–1919." *Public Health Reports,* vol. 125, Supplement 3 (2010): "Influenza Pandemic in the United States," 82–91. www.ncbi.nih.gov/pmc/articles/PMC2862337.

Canavan, Barbara C. "Collaboration Across the Pond: Influenza Virus Research, Interwar United States and Britain." Rockefeller Archive Center Research Reports, December 31, 2014, 3–4. www.rockarch.org/publications/resrep/canavan.pdf.

Centers for Disease Control and Prevention. *Pandemic Influenza—Past, Present, Future: Communicating Today Based on the Lessons from the 1918–1919 Influenza Pandemic. Workshop Proceedings,* October 17, 2006. www.flu.gov/pandemic/workshop.pdf.

―――. "We Heard the Bells: The Influenza of 1918." www.flu.gov/pandemic/history/weheardthebells/script_120709.html.

Ciovacco, Carl J. "The Erosion of Non-combatant Immunity Within Al Qaeda." Small Wars Journal. smallwarsjournal.com/blog/journal/docs-temp/67-ciovacco.pdf.

Collier, Richard. *The Plague of the Spanish Lady: The Influenza Pandemic of 1918–1919.* New York: Atheneum, 1974.

Councell, Clara E. "War and Infectious Disease." *Public Health Reports (1896–1970),* 56, no. 12 (March 21, 1941), 547–573.

Cox, Francis. "The First World War: Disease the Only Victor." Gresham College, London. Lecture, March 10, 2014. www.gresham.ac.uk/lectures-and-events/the-first-world-war-disease-the-only-victor.

Crawford, Dorothy H. *The Invisible Enemy: A Natural History of Viruses.* New York: Oxford University Press, 2000.

―――. *Viruses: A Very Short Introduction.* New York: Oxford University Press, 2011.

Crosby, Alfred W. *America's Forgotten Pandemic: The Influenza of 1918.* 1976. Reprint, New York: Cambridge University Press, 1989.

Cummings, Sarah. "Spanish Influenza Outbreak, 1918." International World History Project. history-world.org/spanish_influenza_of_1918.htm.

Dallas, Gregor. *1918: War and Peace.* New York: Overlook Press, 2001.

Davies, Pete. *Catching Cold: The Hunt for a Killer Virus.* New York: Penguin Books, 2000.

Defoe, Daniel. *A Journal of the Plague Year.* 1722. Reprint, Thorndike, ME: G. K. Hall, 2000.

Deming, Dorothy. "Influenza—1918: Reliving the Great Epidemic." *American Journal of Nursing,* 57, no. 10 (October 1957), 1308–1309.

Diamond, Jared. *Guns, Germs, and Steel: The Fates of Human Societies.* New York: Norton, 1999.

―――. "The Worst Mistake in the History of the Human Race." *Discover,* May 1987.

Duncan, Kirsty. *Hunting the 1918 Flu.* Toronto: University of Toronto Press, 2003.

Eksteins, Modris. *Rites of Spring: The Great War and the Birth of the Modern Age.* Boston: Houghton Mifflin, 1989.

Ellis, Edward Robb. *Echoes of Distant Thunder: Life in the United States, 1914–1918.* New York: Coward, McCann & Geoghegan, 1975.

Erkoreka, Anton. "Origins of the Spanish Influenza Pandemic (1918–1919) and Its Relation to the First World War." *Journal of Molecular and Genetic Medicine,* 3, no. 2 (December 2009), 190–194.

Ewald, Paul W. *Evolution of Infectious Disease.* New York: Oxford University Press, 1994.

Eyler, John M. "The State of Science, Microbiology, and Vaccines Circa 1918." *Public Health Reports,* vol. 125, Supplement 3 (2010): "Influenza Pandemic in the United States," 27–36. www.ncbi.nih.gov/pmc/articles/PMC286332.

Fernandez, Elizabeth. "The Virus Detective: Dr. John Hultin Has Found Evidence of the 1918 Flu Epidemic That Has Eluded Experts for Decades." *San Francisco Chronicle,* February 17, 2002. www.sfgate.com/magazine/article/The-Virus-detective-Dr-John-Hultin-has-found-2872017.php.

Flexner, Simon, and James Thomas Flexner. *William Henry Welch and the Heroic Age of American Medicine.* New York: Viking Press, 1941.

French, Herbert. "The Clinical Features of the Influenza Epidemic of 1918–19." In Ministry of Health of Great Britain, *Report on the Pandemic of Influenza, 1918–19.* London: His Majesty's Stationery Office, 1920.

Garrett, Laurie. "The Bioterrorist Next Door." *Foreign Policy,* December 15, 2011. foreignpolicy.com/2011/12/15/the-bioterrorist-next-door.

———. "The Next Pandemic?" *Foreign Affairs,* July–August 2005. www.foreignaffairs.com/articles/2005-07-01/next-pandemic.

Giffin, Frederick C. "Billy Sunday: The Evangelist as 'Patriot.'" *Social Science,* 48, no. 4 (Autumn 1973), 216–221.

Gilbert, Martin. *The First World War: A Complete History.* New York: Henry Holt, 1994.

Gladwell, Malcolm. "The Dead Zone." *The New Yorker,* September 29, 1997, gladwell.com/the-dead-zone.

Grady, Denise, and Donald G. McNeil Jr., "Debate Persists on Deadly Flu Made Airborne." *New York Times,* December 26, 2011. www.nytimes.com/2011/12/27/science/debate-persists-on-deadly-flu-made-airborne.html?_r=0.

Grist, Roy. "Flu Epidemic of 1918." Digital History. www.digitalhistory.uh.edu/disp_textbook.cfm?smtID=3&psid=1112

Halevi, Jonathan D. "Al-Qaeda's Intellectual Legacy: New Radical Islamic Thinking Justifying Genocide of Infidels." *Jerusalem Viewpoints,* December 1, 2003. www.jcpa.org/jl/vp508.htm.

Hanson, Neil. *Unknown Soldiers: The Story of the Missing of the First World War.* New York: Vintage Books, 2007.

Hartesveldt, Fred R. van. "The Doctors and the 'Flu': The British Medical Profession's Response to the Influenza Pandemic of 1918–19." *International Social Sciences Review,* 85, nos. 1–2 (Spring–Summer 2010), 28–39.

Hays, J. N. *The Burdens of Disease: Epidemics and Human Response in Western History.* New Brunswick, NJ: Rutgers University Press, 2009.

————. *Epidemics and Pandemics: Their Impacts on Human History.* Santa Barbara, CA: ABC-CLIO, 2005.

Hoehling, A. A. *The Great Epidemic.* Boston: Little, Brown, 1961.

Honigsbaum, Mark. *Living with Enza: The Forgotten Story of Britain and the Great Flu Pandemic of 1918.* London: Macmillan, 2009.

Howard, N. P. "The Social and Political Consequences of the Allied Food Blockade of Germany, 1918–19." libcom.org/files/blockade%20Germany_0.pdf.

Humphries, Mark Osborne. "Paths of Infection: The First World War and the Origins of the 1918 Influenza Pandemic." *War in History,* 21, no. 1 (January 2014), 55–81.

Iezzoni, Lynette. *Influenza 1918: The Worst Epidemic in American History.* New York: TV Books, 1999.

"Influenza 1918." *American Experience.* Complete program transcript. PBS. www.pbs.org/wgbh /americanexperience/features/transcript/influenza-transcript.

Jenkins, Philip. *The Great and Holy War: How World War I Became a Religious Crusade.* San Francisco: HarperOne, 2014.

Johnson, Niall, and Juergen Muller. "Updating the Accounts: Global Mortality of the 1918–1920 'Spanish' Influenza Pandemic." *Bulletin of the History of Medicine,* 76 (2002), 105–115.

Karlen, Arno. *Man and Microbes: Disease and Plagues in History and Modern Times.* New York: Simon & Schuster, 1996.

Keeling, Arlene W. "'Alert to the Necessities of the Emergency': U.S. Nursing During the 1918 Influenza Pandemic." *Public Health Reports,* vol. 125, Supplement 3 (2010): "Influenza Pandemic in the United States," 105–112. www.ncbi.nih.gov/pmc/articles/PMC2862339.

Kelly, John. *The Great Mortality: An Intimate History of the Black Death, the Most Devastating Plague of All Time.* New York: HarperCollins, 2005.

Kennedy, David M. *Over Here: The First World War and American Society.* New York: Oxford University Press, 1980.

Kilbourne, Edwin D. "Influenza Pandemics of the 20th Century." *Emerging Infectious Diseases,* 12, no. 1 (January 2006), 9–14. wwwnc.cdc.gov/eid/article/12/1/05-1254_article.

Killingray, David. "The Influenza Pandemic of 1918–1919 in the British Caribbean." *Social History of Medicine,* 7, no. 1 (April 1994), 59–87.

Kolata, Gina Bari. *Flu: The Story of the Great Influenza Epidemic of 1918 and the Search for the Virus That Caused It.* New York: Farrar, Straus and Giroux, 1999.

Koszarski, Richard. "Flu Season: *Moving Picture World* Reports on Pandemic Influenza, 1918–19." *Film History,* 17, no. 4 (2005), 466–485.

Kraut, Alan M. "Immigration, Ethnicity, and the Pandemic." *Public Health Reports,* vol. 125, Supplement 3 (2010): "Influenza Pandemic in the United States," 123–133. www.ncbi.nih.gov /pmc/articles/PMC2862341.

————. *Silent Travelers: Germs, Genes, and the "Immigrant Menace."* New York: Basic Books, 1994.

Kreiser, Christine M. "1918 Spanish Influenza Outbreak: The Enemy Within." History Net, October 27, 2006. www.historynet.com/1918-spanish-influenza-outbreak-the-enemy-within .htm.

Langford, Christopher. "Did the 1918–19 Influenza Pandemic Originate in China?" *Population and Development Review,* 31, no. 3 (September 2005), 473–505.

Lu, Alicia. "Why Publishing a Bird Flu–Human Transmission Guide Was an Incredibly Dumb Idea." *Bustle,* April 11, 2014. www.bustle.com/articles/20893-why-publishing-a-bird-flu -human-transmission-guide-was-an-incredibly-dumb-idea.

Macdonald, Lyn. *The Roses of No Man's Land.* New York: Atheneum, 1989.

————. *Somme.* London: Michael Joseph, 1983.

MacMillan, Margaret. *Peacemakers: The Paris Conference of 1919 and Its Attempt to End War.* London: John Murray, 2001.

Marsh, Patricia. "'Mysterious Malady Spreading': Press Coverage of the 1918–19 Influenza Pandemic in Ireland." *Quest Proceedings of the QUB AHSS Conference June 2008,* 6 (Autumn 2008), 169, 171. www.qub.ac/uk/quest.

McCullough, David. *Truman.* New York: Simon & Schuster, 1992.

McNeill, William H. *Plagues and Peoples.* Garden City, NY: Anchor Press, 1976.

Moore, Kirsten. "Medical Manipulation: Public Health as a Political Tool in the 1918–19 Influenza Epidemic in San Francisco." *Voces Novae,* 3, no. 1 (2011). journals.chapman.edu/ojs/index.php /VocesNovae/article/view/212/545.

Morgan, David T. "The Revivalist as Patriot: Billy Sunday and World War I." *Journal of Presbyterian History (1962–1985),* 51, no. 2 (Summer 1973), 199–215.

Morrisey, Carla R. "The Influenza Epidemic of 1918." *Navy Medicine,* 77, no. 3 (May–June 1986), 11–17. www.ibiblio.org/hyperwar/AMH/XX/WWI/flu/flu1918/flu1918.html.

Mulligan, William. *The Great War for Peace.* New Haven, CT: Yale University Press, 2014.

Navarro, Julian A. "Influenza in 1918: An Epidemic in Images." *Public Health Reports,* vol. 125, Supplement 3 (2010): "Influenza Pandemic in the United States," 9–14. www.ncbi.nih.gov /pmc/articles/PMC2862330.

Nikiforuk, Andrew. *Pandemonium: Bird Flu, Mad Cow Disease and Other Biological Plagues of the 21st Century.* Toronto: Viking Canada, 2006.

Oldstone, Michael B. A. *Viruses, Plagues and History.* New York: Oxford University Press, 1998.

Oxford, J. S., et al. "A Hypothesis: The Conjunction of Soldiers, Gas, Pigs, Ducks, Geese and Horses in Northern France During the Great War Provided the Conditions for the Emergence of the 'Spanish' Influenza Pandemic of 1918–1919." *Vaccine,* 23, no. 7 (January 4, 2005), 940–945.

Parry, Wynne. "Killer-Flu Debate: Should Mutant H5N1 Have Been Created?" Live Science, December 23, 2011. www.livescience.com/17623-deadly-h5n1-virus-recipe-debate.html.

Persico, Joseph E. *Eleventh Month, Eleventh Day, Eleventh Hour: Armistice Day, 1918—World War I and Its Violent Climax.* New York: Random House, 2004.

———. "The Great Swine Flu Epidemic of 1918." *American Heritage Magazine,* 27, no. 4 (June 1976). www.americanheritage.com/print/53422.

Pettit, Dorothy A., and Janice Bailie. *A Cruel Wind: Pandemic Flu in America, 1918–1920.* Murfreesboro, TN: Timberlane Books, 2008.

Phillips, Howard. *Black October: The Impact of the Spanish Influenza Epidemic of 1918 on South Africa.* Pretoria, South Africa: Government Printer, 1990.

———. "Influenza Pandemic." *International Encyclopedia of the First World War.* encyclopedia.1914-1918-online.net/article/influenza_pandemic.

———. "Influenza Pandemic (Africa)." *International Encyclopedia of the First World War.* encyclopedia.1914-1918-online.net/article/influenza_pandemic_africa.

———. "The Recent Wave of 'Spanish' Flu Historiography." *Social History of Medicine,* 27, no. 4 (2014), 789–808. www.historicalstudies.uct.ac.za/ . . . /Phillips%20-%SHOM%20-%20The . . .

———. "Why Did It Happen? Religious Explanations of the 'Spanish' Flu Epidemic in South Africa." *Historically Speaking,* 9, no. 7 (September–October 2008), 34–36.

Porter, Roy. *The Greatest Benefit to Mankind: A Medical History of Humanity.* New York: Norton, 1997.

Potter, C. W. "A History of Influenza." *Journal of Applied Microbiology,* 91, no. 4 (October 2001), 572–579.

Quammen, David. "The Next Pandemic: Not If, but When." *New York Times,* May 9, 2013.

Quinn, Tom. *Flu: A Social History of Influenza.* London: New Holland Publishers, 2008.

Raico, Ralph. "The Blockade and Attempted Starvation of Germany." Mises Daily, May 7, 2010. mises.org/library/blockade-and-attempted-starvation-germany.

Rosen, William. *Justinian's Flea: Plague, Empire, and the Birth of Europe.* New York: Viking, 2007.

Russell, Francis. "A Journal of the Plague: The 1918 Influenza." In *The Great Interlude: Neglected Events and Persons from the First World War to the Depression.* New York: McGraw-Hill, 1964.

Sherman, Irwin W. *Twelve Diseases That Changed Our World.* Washington, DC: ASM Press, 2007.

Smallman-Raynor, Matthew R., and Andrew D. Cliff. "Impact of Infectious Diseases on War." *Infectious Disease Clinics of North America,* 18 (2004), 341–368.

Smith, Larry. "A Hurricane Across the Green Fields of Life: How the 1918 Flu Affected the Caribbean." Bahama Pundit, October 26, 2005. www.bahamapundit.com/2005/10/how _the_1918_fl_1.html.

Speckhard, Anne. "The New Global Jihad, 9-11, and the Use of Weapons of Mass Destruction: Changes in Mindset and Modus Operandi." theclaw.typepad.com.speckhard_vault/files /Al_Qaeda.pdf.

Specter, Michael. "The Deadliest Virus." *The New Yorker,* March 12, 2012. www.newyorker.com /magazine/2012/03/12/the-deadliest-virus.

————. "The Doomsday Strain." *The New Yorker,* December 20 and 27, 2010. www.newyorker .com/magazine/2010/12/20/the-doomsday-strain.

————. "Nature's Bioterrorist." *The New Yorker,* February 28, 2005. www.newyorker.com /magazine/2005/02/28/natures-bioterrorist-2.

Stern, Alexandra Minna, et al. " 'Better Off in School': School Medical Inspection as a Public Health Strategy During the 1918–1919 Influenza Pandemic in the United States." *Public Health Reports,* vol. 125, Supplement 3 (2010): "Influenza Pandemic in the United States," 63–70. www.ncbi.nih.gov/pmc/articles/PMC2862335.

Summers, Jennifer A. "Pandemic Influenza Outbreak on a Troop Ship—Diary of a Soldier in 1918." *Emerging Infectious Diseases,* 18, no. 11 (November 2012). wwwnc.cdc.gov/eid /article/18/11/ad-1811_article.

Taubenberger, Jeffery K. "Influenza: Trying to Catch a Moving Target." *Scientific American,* November 11, 2013. www.scientificamerican.com/article/influenza-trying-to-catch-a-moving -target.

————. Interview by *American Experience,* PBS, January 1998. www.pbs.org/wgbh /americanexperience/features/interview/influenza-jeffrey-taubenberger.

————. "Jeffery Taubenberger—Full Transcript." Conversations with Pathologists. Interview, November 27, 2007. www.pathsoc.org/conversations/index.php?view=article&catid=65%3A jeffery-taubenberger&id=92%3Ajeffery-taubenberger-full-transcript&option=com_contents.

Taubenberger, Jeffery, et al. "Reconstruction of the 1918 Influenza Virus: Unexpected Rewards from the Past." *mBio,* 3, no. 5 (September 11, 2012), e00201–212. mbio.asm.org/content/3/5 /e00201-12.full.pdf.

Taubenberger, Jeffery, and David M. Morens. "1918 Influenza: The Mother of All Pandemics." *Emerging Infectious Diseases,* 12, no. 1 (January 2006). wwwnc.cdc.gov/eid/article/12/1/05-0979 _article.

Taubenberger, Jeffery, Ann H. Reid, and Thomas G. Fanning. "Capturing a Killer Flu Virus." *Scientific American,* January 2005. www.scientificamerican.com/article/capturing-a-killer-flu -virus.

Tomes, Nancy. " 'Destroyer and Teacher': Managing the Masses During the 1918–1919 Influenza Pandemic." *Public Health Reports,* vol. 125, Supplement 3 (2010): "Influenza Pandemic in the United States," 48–62. www.ncbi.nih.gov/pmc/articles/PMC2862334.

————. "The Making of a Germ Panic, Then and Now." *American Journal of Public Health,* 90, no. 2 (February 2002), 191–198.

Trilla, Antonio. "The 1918 'Spanish Flu' in Spain." *Clinical Infectious Diseases,* 47, no. 5 (2008), 668–673.

Trueman, C. N. "November 11th 1918." History Learning Site, March 6, 2015. www.historylearningsite.co.uk/world-war-one/november-11th-1918.

Tschanz, David W. "Plague of the Spanish Lady." MilitaryHistoryOnline.com, December 11, 2011.www.militaryhistoryonline.com/wwi/articles/plagueofspanishlady.aspx.

Vaughan, Victor C. *A Doctor's Memories.* Indianapolis: Bobbs-Merrill, 1926.

Vergano, Dan. "1918 Flu Pandemic That Killed 50 Million Originated in China, Historians Say." *National Geographic,* January 24, 2014. news/nationalgeographic.com/news/2014/01/140123 -spanish-flu-1918-china-origins-pandemic-science-health.

Watson, Alexander. *Ring of Steel: Germany and Austria-Hungary at War, 1914–1918.* New York: Penguin Books, 2015.

Wedeking, Rachel. "Oral History with Ms. Josie Mabel Brown." Washington, DC: Office of Medical History, Bureau of Medicine and Surgery, 1986. www.med.navy.mil.bumed/nm history/Oral%20Histories2/BROWN%20Josie%20%Mabel.pdf.

White, Kenneth A. "Pittsburgh in the Great Epidemic of 1918." *Western Pennsylvania Historical Magazine,* 68, no. 3 (July 1985), 221–242.

Zimmer, Carl. *A Planet of Viruses.* Chicago: University of Chicago Press, 2011.

PICTURE CREDITS

INDEX